I0023641

John McCaskey

Franklin Square song collection, no. 2

Two hundred favorite songs and hymns for schools and homes, nursery and fireside

John McCaskey

Franklin Square song collection, no. 2
Two hundred favorite songs and hymns for schools and homes, nursery and fireside

ISBN/EAN: 9783337175818

Printed in Europe, USA, Canada, Australia, Japan

Cover: Foto ©Thomas Meinert / pixelio.de

More available books at **www.hansebooks.com**

Franklin Square Song Collection:

Two Hundred

Favorite Songs and Hymns for Schools and Homes, Nursery and Fireside.

No. 2.

SELECTED BY J. P. McCASKEY.

I was once at a little musical party in New York, where several accomplished amateur singers were present, and with them the eminent professional, Adelaide Phillips. The amateurs were first called. Each chose some difficult operatic passage, and sang her best. When it came to the great singer's turn, instead of exhibiting her ability to eclipse these rivals on her own ground, she simply seated herself at the piano and sang 'Kathleen Mavourneen,' with such thrilling sweetness, that the young Irish girl who was setting the supper-table in the next room forgot her plates and teaspoons, threw herself into a chair, put her apron over her face, and sobbed as if her heart would break.—*Thos. W. Higginson.*

NEW YORK

HARPER & BROTHERS, FRANKLIN SQUARE.

I T " lacks orderly arrangement " has been an occasional criticism upon the First Number. It pretends to none; but is simply a collection of good things brought together, with reading matter, pertinent and suggestive, sandwiched between—the singer or reader taking what he finds " for better, for worse." While in No. 1 everything is complete on its own page, in No. 2 no leaf is turned to complete any Song or Hymn. There is no space lost or wasted anywhere, unless, indeed, matter of no value has at times found place here, which we trust will not be the verdict of many who may use this Second Number. That the book may be as useful and as satisfactory as possible, the selections are arranged, with few exceptions, in four parts, so that they can be sung or played in solo, duet, trio, or quartette, according to circumstances, or as may be preferred for voices or instruments. Some, of course, are best as solos, others in two, three, or four parts, or in the full-voiced harmony of the great chorus.

Special acknowledgments are made to Publishers and others for copyright privileges and numerous favors. To Prof. CARL MATZ, who verifies the saying, " When you find a Prussian you find a man," the Compiler cannot express too heartily his sense of personal obligation. Endowed with the divine gift of harmony in an extraordinary degree, possessed of exquisite taste, and a power of memory in music that is phenomenal, to this he has superadded the rigid training of the best schools of music in the world. He is a graduate of the first rank from the famous Seminary of Kœpenick, near Berlin, where for the third year of the course, (1866), under Rudolph Lange, he was leader of the grand orchestra and of the chorus of a hundred voices, having been chosen conductor by vote of the students of music in recognition of his eminent ability. He was then, for a year, connected with the Stern Institute, the Royal Conservatory of Berlin, after which he had charge of one of the finest organs in Germany for upwards of two years before coming to America. Since that time he has led a very busy life as conductor and organist, choir instructor, and teacher of music in public and private schools. Thus much in evidence that the harmony here found is approved by, or is from the hand of, a master.

All persons who enjoy music have their favorite Songs and Hymns, and some into whose hands this Collection may fall, would be pleased to find such favorites here. If they will address the Compiler, in care of the Publishers, suggesting the names of such old pieces as they remember pleasantly, sending copies of the same or stating where they may be found, they will be carefully considered, and the merits of the book as a Popular Collection will be much enhanced.

Contents of Song Collection.

SONG COLLECTION.

MY MOTHER'S BIBLE.

HENRY RUSSELL.
GEORGE P. MORRIS.

1. This book is all that's left me now! Tears will un-bid-den start; With
2. Ah! well do I re-mem-ber those Whose names these rec-ords bear: Who
3. My fa-ther read this ho-ly book To broth-ers, sis-ters dear; How
4. Thou true-est friend man ev-er knew, Thy con-stan-cy I've tried; Where

falt-'ring lip and throb-bing brow, I press it to my heart. For
round the hearth-stone used to close Af-ter the ev'-ning prayer. And
calm was my poor moth-er's look, Who leaned God's word to hear. Her
all were false, I found thee true, My coun-sel-lor and guide. The

ma-ny gen-er-a-tions past, Here is our fam-'ly tree; My
speak of what these pa-ges said, In tones my heart would thrill! Tho'
an-gel face—I see it yet! What throng-ing mem-'ries come! A-
mines of earth no treas-ure give That could this vol-ume buy; In

rit.

mo-ther's hands this Bi-ble clasped; She, dy-ing, gave it me.
they are with the si-lent dead, Here are they liv-ing still.
gain that lit-tle group is met With-in the halls of home.
teach-ing me the way to live, It taught me how to die.

CARE OF THE VOICE.—Mr. Eichberg, Supervisor of Music in the public schools of Boston, gives the following caution, which is well worth heeding. He says: The age of most of the pupils in the high schools renders extreme caution in the treatment of their voices a duty and a sacred obligation. The common belief that boys' voices alone require especial care during the period of transition has led to much loss of voice and of health. Just as important, if less striking, changes occur in the nature and 'timbre' of the female voice. I am convinced that the voice of a girl from twelve to seventeen years of age requires all the more careful management from the very fact that, not suffering, like a boy, from an almost absolute impossibility to sing, she is likely to over-exert herself, to the lasting injury of both health and voice. When teachers are better acquainted with these physiological facts, they will understand the necessity of not sacrificing such young—such temporarily "diseased" voices—to the

DO THEY THINK OF ME AT HOME?

J. E. CARPENTER.
CHAS. W. GLOVER.

Do they think of me at home, Do they ev - er think of me? I who
Do they think of me at eve? Of the songs I used to sing? Is the
Do they think of how I loved In my hap - py, ear - ly days? Do they

shared their ev - 'ry grief, I who min-gled in their glee? Have their hearts grown cold and
harp I struck untouch'd, Does a stranger wake the string? Will no kind for - giv-ing
think of him who came, But could nev - er win their praise? I am hap - py by his

strange To the one now doom'd to roam, I would give the world to know,—"Do they
word Come a-cross the rag - ing foam? Shall I nev - er cease to sigh,— " Do they
side, And from mine he'll nev - er roam, But my heart will sad - ly ask,— "Do they

think of me at home?" I would give the world to know, "Do they think of me at home?"
think of me at home?" Shall I nev - er cease to sigh, "Do they think of me at home?"
think of me at home?" But my heart will sad - ly ask, "Do they think of me at home?"

desire of exhibiting and showing off their classes. Another frightful cause of injury proceeds from the desire of many female pupils always to sing the highest part—the first soprano. It is with them "*Aut Cæsar, aut nullus.*" Periodical examination of the pupils' voices, by the teacher, has seemed to me the only safe course in order to remedy this evil. In Jenny Lind's younger days, it is related that she applied for instructions to Garcia, the great teacher of vocal music in Paris. He heard her sing, and then told her her voice was gone, that she must not sing a note for a year, and return to him at the end of that time, and in the meantime improve her health. She faithfully complied with these directions, and came back to Garcia at the appointed time. Rest at a critical period, had restored her voice, to her own delight and to the gratification of her master. From that moment a grand career was open before her, which has made her name a "household word" in two continents.

THE MELLOW HORN.

Wm. Jones.

1. At dawn Auro - ra gai - ly breaks, In all her proud attire, Ma - jes - tic o'er the glassy lake, Re-
2. At eve when gloomy shades obscure The tranquil shepherd's cot, When tinkling bells are heard no more, And

fleet - ing li - quid fire; All na - ture smiles to ush - er in The blushing queen of morn, And
dai - ly toil for - get, 'Tis then the sweet enchanting note On zephyrs gent - ly borne, With

hunts - men with the day be - gin To wind the mel - low horn. The mel - low horn, The
witch - ing ca - dence seems to float A - round the mel - low horn. The mel - low horn, The

mel - low, mel - low horn; The mel - low horn, The mel - low, mel - low horn; And
mel - low, mel - low horn; The mel - low horn, The mel - low, mel - low horn; 'Tis

hunts - men with the day begin To wind the mellow horn. And huntsmen with the day begin To
then the sweet enchanting note On zephyrs gently borne : With witching cadence seems to float A-

wind the mellow horn. The mellow, mellow horn, The mel low, mellow horn.
round the mellow horn. The mellow, mellow horn, The mel - low, mellow horn.

* An Echo can be made by Soprano and Alto humming these two bars to this note, with lips closed and teeth apart.

MUSICAL HEREDITY.—Heredity shows itself more markedly, it would seem, in the arts than in the sciences. Taking music we find some remarkable instances. The Bach family, which took its rise about 1550 and became extinct in 1800, presents an unbroken series of musicians for nearly two centuries. The head of the family was a baker of Presburg, his two sons were the first who were musicians by profession. Their descendants "overran Thuringia, Saxony, and Franconia," says Papillon. "They were all organists, church singers, or what is called in Germany, 'city musicians.' When they became too numerous to live all together, and the members of this family were scattered abroad, they resolved to meet once a year, on a stated day, with a view to maintaining a sort of patriarchal bond of union. This custom was kept up until nearly the middle of the eighteenth century, and oftentimes more than a 100 persons bearing the name of Bach—men, women, and children—were to be seen assembled. In the family are reckoned twenty-nine eminent musicians, and twenty-eight of a lower grade." Rossini's family

SPEAK GENTLY.

D. BATES.
W. V. WALLACE.

1. Speak gen-tly— it is bet-ter far   To rule by love than fear;   Speak gen-tly—let no harsh word mar   The good we may do here. Speak gen-tly to the lit-tle child! Its love be sure   to gain; Teach it in ac-cents soft and mild,   It may not long re-main,   Teach it in accents soft and mild, It may not long re-main.

2. Speak gen-tly to the young—for they   Will have e-nough to bear;   Pass through this life as best they may,   'Tis full of anx-ious care. Speak gen-tly to the ag-ed one, Grieve not the care-worn heart, Whose sands of life are near-ly run;   Let such in peace de-part,   Whose sands of life are nearly run,   Let such in peace de-part.

3. Speak gen-tly to the err-ing, know   They must have toiled in vain;   Per-haps unkindness made them so;   Oh, win them back a-gain. Speak gen-tly, 'tis a lit-tle thing Dropped in the heart's deep well; The good, the joy, that it may bring, E-ter-ni-ty shall tell,   The good, the joy, that it may bring, E-ter-ni-ty shall tell.

rit.

often played music at fairs; Beethoven's father and grandfather were musicians; Mozart's father was Capellmeister to the Bishop of Saltzburg.—*Cornhill.*

IT is night now, and here is home. Gathered under the quiet roof, elders and children lie, alike at rest. In the midst of a great calm the stars look out from the heavens. The silence is peopled with the past—sorrowful remorse for sins and short-comings, memories of passionate joys and griefs rise out of their graves, both now alike calm and sad. Eyes, as I shut mine, look at me that have long since ceased to shine. The town and the fair landscape sleep under the starlight, wreathed under the Autumn mist. Twinkling among the houses, a light keeps watch here and there, in what may be a sick chamber or two. The clock tolls sweetly in the silent air. Here is night and rest. An awful sense of thanks makes the heart swell and the head bow, as I pass to my room through the sleeping house, and feel as though a hushed blessing were upon it.—*Thackeray.*

GOOD NIGHT.

Moderato.

VOLKSLIED.

1. How soft the hap - py even - ing's close, 'Tis the hour for sweet repose, Good
2. These tran - quil hours of so - cial mirth, Form the dear - est ties of earth: Good
3. Oh, how each gen - tle thought is stirred, As we breathe the parting word: Good

night! The sum - mer winds have sunk to rest, The moon se - rene - ly bright, Sheds
night! And while each hand is kind - ly pressed, Oh, may our pray'rs to heaven, With
night! Could we but ev - er feel as now, Our hearts with love up - raised, And

dim. *ril.*

down her calm and gen - tle ray, Soft - ly now she seems to say, Good night!
hum - ble fer - vor be ad - dressed, For its bless - ings on our rest: Good night!
while our fond af - fec - tions flow, Hear in mur - murs soft and low—Good night!

THE BETTER WISH.

HENRY RUSSELL.

R. R. If I had but a thousand a year, Gaf-fer Green, If I had but a thousand a
G. G. The best wish you could have, take my word, Robin Ruff, Would scare find you in bread or in

year! What a man would I be, And what sights would I see, If I
beer; But be hon - est and true, And say what would you do, If you

had but a thou- sand a year, Gaf- fer Green, If I had but a thousand a year!
had but a thou- sand a year, Rob-in Ruff? If you had but a thousand a year!

R. I would do, I scarcely know what, Gaffer Green,
    I would go, faith! I hardly know where,
      I would scatter the chink
      And leave others to think,
    If I had but a thousand a year, Gaffer Green!
    If I had but a thousand a year!

G. But when you are aged and grey, Robin Ruff,
    And the day of your death it draws near,
      Say, what with your pains
      Would you do with your gains,
    If you then had a thousand a year, Robin Ruff?
    If you then had a thousand a year?

R. I scarcely can tell what you mean, Gaffer Green,
    For your questions are always so queer,
      But as other folks die,
      I suppose so must I— [Ruff?
G. What! and give up your thousand a year, Robin
    And give up your thousand a year?

There's a place that is better than this, Robin Ruff,
    And I hope in my heart you'll go there,
      Where the poor man's as great,
R.   What! though he hath no estate?
G. Yes, as if he'd a thousand a year, Robin Ruff,
G. & R. Yes, as if he'd a thousand a year.

THE EAR.—The sound-wave passes first into the auditory canal, about an inch in length, and striking against the tympanum, or ear-drum, which closes the orifice of the external ear, it throws this membrane into vibration. Next, a series of small bones, called respectively, from their peculiar form, the *hammer, anvil,* and *stirrup,* conduct to the inner ear, which is termed, from its complicated stucture, the *labyrinth.* This is filled with liquid, and contains semi-circular canals, and the cochlea (snailshell) which receive the vibrations and transmit them to the auditory nerve, the fine filaments of which are spread out to catch every pulsation of the sound-wave. The middle ear, which contains the chain of small bones, is a simple cavity about half an inch in diameter, filled with air. It communicates with the mouth by means of the Eustachian tube. Within the labyrinth are also fine, elastic hair-bristles and crystalline particles among the nerve-fibres, wonderfully fitted, the one to receive and the other to prolong the vibrations; and lastly, a lute of 3,000 microscopic strings, so stretched as to vibrate in uni-

WHY DO SUMMER ROSES FADE?

GEORGE BARKER.

Why do sum-mer ros-es fade? If not to show how fleet-ing,
Then while sum-mer ros-es last, Oh, let's be friends to-geth-er,
But though sum-mer ros-es die, And love gives place to rea-son,

All things bright and fair are made, To bloom awhile as half a-fraid To join our sum-mer
Sum-mer time will soon be past, With au-tumn leaves around us cast, And then comes win-try
Friendship pass without a sigh, And all on earth pass coldly by; 'Tis but a win-try

greet-ing? Or do they on-ly bloom to tell, How brief a sea-son
weath-er. Sure-ly as the sum mer's day, Friend-ship, too, will
sea-son, And friendship, love and ros-es too, The spring-time shall a-

love may dwell, Or do they on-ly bloom to tell, How brief a sea-son love may dwell?
pass a-way, Sure-ly as the sum-mer's day, Friendship too will pass a-way.
gain re-new, And friendship, love and ros-es too, The spring-time shall a-gain re-new,

son with any sound. The Eustachian tube is generally closed, thus cutting off the air in the inner cavity from the external air. If at any time the pressure of the atmosphere without becomes greater or less than that within, the tympanum feels the strain. A forcible blow upon the ear may produce in this way temporary deafness. In the act of swallowing, the tube is opened and the equilibrium restored. We may force air into the cavity of the ear by closing our mouth and nose, and forcibly expiring the air from our lungs. This will render us insensible to low sounds, while we can hear the higher ones as usual.—*Steele.*

A tired bee hums in E; while in pursuit of honey it hums contentedly in A. The common horse-fly, when held captive, moves its wings 335 times a second; a honey-bee, 190 times. Youmans says it is marvelous how slight an impulse throws a vast amount of air into motion. We can easily hear the song of a bird 500 feet above us. For its melody to reach us it must have filled with wave pulsations a sphere of air, one thousand feet in diameter, or set in motion eighteen tons of the atmosphere.

BEULAH LAND.

Edgar Page.
J. R. Sweney, by per.

1. I've reached the land of corn and wine, And all its rich-es freely mine; Here shines undimm'd one
2. The Saviour comes and walks with me, And sweet communion here have we; He gent-ly leads me
3. A sweet per-fume up-on the breeze Is borne from ever-ver-nal trees, And flow'rs that never
4. The zephyrs seem to float to me, Sweet sounds of heaven's mel-o-dy, As an-gels with the

bliss-ful day, For all my night has pass'd a-way.
with His hand, For this is Heaven's bor-der-land.
fad-ing grow Where streams of life for-ev-er flow.
white-robed throng, Join in the sweet redemption song.

Oh, Beu-lah land, sweet Beulah land, As

on thy highest mount I stand, I look a-way a-cross the sea, Where mansions are pre-

pared for me, And view the shin-ing glo-ry shore, My heav'n, my home, for-ev-'er-more.

ALL HAIL THE POWER OF JESUS' NAME.

F. Perronet, 1780.
O. Holden, 1793. "Coronation."

1. All hail the power of Je-sus' name! Let angels prostrate fall; Bring forth the royal di-a-dem, And
2. Sinners, whose love can ne'er forget The wormwood and the gall, Go, spread your trophies at His feet, And
3. Let ev'ry kindred, ev'ry tribe, On this ter-res-trial ball, To Him all ma-jes-ty as-cribe, And

crown Him Lord of all; Bring forth the royal di-a-dem, And crown Him Lord of all.
crown Him Lord of all; Go, spread your trophies at His feet, And crown Him Lord of all.
crown Him Lord of all; To Him all ma-jes-ty as-cribe And crown Him Lord of all.

TOO ARTISTIC.—The great mistake as to the singing in public worship is the desire to make it artistic. In Rome and Paris people rush to the churches to hear the singing; they care nothing for the other parts of the mass. Such is the case in many Protestant churches, where devotional singing has given way to the operatic. We have heard of a church where the preaching is voted a bore, but where the fashionable resort to hear sacred songs sung by professional singers from the opera; where the singing costs more than the preaching. How much better is it to go to such churches, where the praying and preaching are mere accompaniments to the singing, than going to the opera? The truth is, that we sacrifice the devotional in the proportion that we cultivate the artistic beyond a given line. People that know not a note in music, can sing the praises of God so as to excite their devotional feelings, if the tune is a familiar one. And these form the great majority of ordinary congregations; and it is in reference to these, and not for the few cultivated ears, that the singing of congregations should be conducted. We heard the choir of the Sistine Chapel, and of St. Peter's and of St. Paul's; but so far as devotion is concerned, their singing bore no comparison to that we have heard in Scotch churches, led by a precentor from a seat under the pulpit; or in a Methodist church, when the brethren had "a good time." The singing in which most of the people can unite, may not be the most tasteful and classical, but is the best for the people; it is the most devotional. It may grate upon the ears of young misses from boarding-

REJOICE, REJOICE.

1. Re - joice! re - joice! the sum-mer months are coming; Re - joice! re - joice! the birds be - gin to sing. When joy bursts forth in songs of praise, And hills re-sound-ing ech - oes raise, When joy bursts forth in songs of praise, And hills re - sounding ech - oes raise.

2. Re - joice! re - joice! the budding flowers are bursting, Re - joice! re - joice! their fra - grance fills the air. When ro - ses bloom and dai - sies grow, And woodbines twine, and vio - lets blow; When ro - ses bloom and dai - sies grow, And woodbines twine and violets blow.

3. Re - joice! re - joice! the sum-mer days are pass - ing, Re - joice! re - joice! their sweets they now im - part, The cool - ing morn, the sun - ny day, Which balmy even - ing wears a - way; The cool - ing morn, the sun - ny day, Which balmy even-ing wears a - way.

schools, and of young gentlemen of operatic tastes; but because it elevates the religious feelings of the people, it is harmony in the ear of heaven. When even soldiers are led to the deadly breach, it is always under the inspiriting influence of words and tunes in which battalions may unite. If the "Marseillaise," as Lamartine says, was to Frenchmen as "a recovered echo from Thermopylæ," why should not our Christian psalms and hymns be so sung as to be recovered echoes from Calvary? As singing is the part of public worship designed to unite all the people in concert it is a desecration of it to surrender it to a committee of artist musicians in the gallery.—*Dr. Murray.*

STRANGE as it may seem, if there were no creature that could hear upon the earth, there would be no such thing as sound, though all the movements in nature were going on just as they are now. Try to grasp this thoroughly, for it is difficult at first to make people believe it. Suppose you were stone-deaf, there would be no such thing as sound to you. A heavy hammer falling on an anvil would indeed shake the air violently, but since this air when it reached your ear would find a useless instrument, could not play upon it. And it is this play on the drum of your ear and the nerves within it speaking to your brain which makes sound. Therefore, if all creatures on or around the earth were without ears or nerves of hearing, there would be no instruments on which to play, and consequently there would be no such thing as sound. This proves that two things are needed in order that we may hear. First, the outside movement which plays on our hearing instrument; and secondly, the hearing instrument itself, of whose structure few people know anything whatever.

HANDEL was one of the most humorous of mortals, and at the same time one of the most irritable. His best jokes were perpetrated frequently during his most violent bursts of passion. Having occasion to bring out one of his oratorios in a provincial town of England, he began to look about for such material to complete his orchestra and chorus as the place might afford. One and another was recommended, as usual, as being a splendid singer, a great player, and so on. After a while these were gathered together in a room, and, after preliminaries, Handel made his appearance, puffing, both arms full of manuscripts. "Gentlemen," quoth he, "you all read manuscripts?" "Yes, yes," responded from all parts of the room. "We play in the church," added an old man behind a violoncello. "Very well, play dis," said Handel, distributing the parts. This done, and a few explanations delivered, Handel retired to a distant part of the room to enjoy the effect. The stumbling, fumbling and blundering that ensued is said to have been indescribable. Handel's sensitive ear and impetuous spirit could not long brook the insult, and clapping his hands to his ears, he ran to the old gentleman of the violoncello, and shaking his fist furiously at the terrified man and the instrument, said, "You blay in de church!—very well—you may blay in de church—for we read, De Lord is long suffering, of great kindness, forgiving iniquity, transgression and sin; you sal blay in de church, but you sal not blay for me!" and snatching together his manuscripts, he rushed out of the room, leaving his astonished performers to draw their own conclusions.

SHELLS OF OCEAN.

J. W. CHERRY. C. MATZ ARR.

With Expression.

1. One sum-mer eve, with pen-sive thought, I wan-der'd on the sea-beat shore, Where oft, in heed-less in-fant sport, I gather'd shells in days be-fore, I gath-er'd shells in days be-fore: The plashing waves like mus-ic fell, Re-spon-sive to my fan-cy wild; A dream came o'er me like a spell, I thought I was a-gain a child, A dream came o'er me like a spell, I thought I was a-gain, a-gain a child.

2. I stoop'd up-on the peb-bly strand, To cull the toys that round me lay, But, as I took them in my hand, I threw them one by one a-way, I threw them one by one a-way: Oh, thus, I said, in ev-'ry stage, By toys our fan-cy is be-guiled; We gather shells from youth to age, And then we leave them, like a child, We gath-er shells from youth to age, And then we leave them, leave them, like a child.

Grace notes to 2d verse.

I HAVE often seen piano-forte players and singers make such strange motions over instrument or song-book, that I have wanted to laugh at them. "Where did our friend pick up these fine ecstatic airs?" I would say to myself. Then I would remember my lady in "marriage a la mode," and amuse myself thinking an affectation was the same thing in Hogarth's time as in our own. But one day I bought me a canary bird and hung it up in a cage at my window. By-and-by he found himself at home, and began to pipe his little tunes; and there he was, sure enough, swimming and waving about, with all the droopings and liftings, languishing side-turnings of the head that I had laughed at. And now I should like to ask who taught him all this?—and me, through him, that the foolish head was not the one swinging itself from side to side and bowing and nodding over the music, but that other which was passing its shallow and self-satisfied judgment on a creature made of finer clay than the stalwart frame which has so very long

HERDSMAN'S MOUNTAIN HOME.

(DER SCHWEIZERBUE.)

CARL MATZ Arr.

1. On the mountain, steep and hoary, Sounds the herdsman's evening song; Where the clouds, in golden glo - ry, Float the am-bient tide a - long, Where the clouds, in gold-en glo - ry, Float the ambient tide a - long. La la la la la la la la la la la la la la la la la la la la la la la la la la la la la.

2. Where the Alpine rose is blowing, Where the herdsman builds his home; From his couch at morning go - ing, With the lark he loves to roam! From his couch at morning go - ing, With the lark he loves to roam! La la la la la la la la la la la la la la la la la la la la la la la la la la la la.

carried that same critical head upon its shoulders?

YOUR former conversation has made me think repeatedly what a number of beautiful words there are of which we never think of estimating the value, as there are of blessings. How carelessly, for example, do we (not we, but people) say "I am delighted to *hear from you.*" No other language has this beautiful expression, which, like some of the most lovely flowers, loses its charm for want of close inspection. When I consider the deep sense of these very simple and very common words, I seem to hear a voice coming from afar through the air, intrusted to the care of the elements, for the nurture of my sympathy.—*Landor.*

WE often hear that this or that "is not worth an old song." Alas! how few things are! What precious recollections do some of them awaken! What pleasurable tears do they excite! They purify the streams of life; they can delay it in its shelves and rapids; they can turn it back again to the soft cool moss amidst which its sources issue.—*Landor.*

SOUND OUR VOICES LONG AND SWEET.

BOHEMIAN MELODY.

Lively. p

1. Sound our voices long and sweet, And roll the stirring drum; Friends and neighbors round us meet, And
2. Now the ro - sy morn is come, Of merry, gladsome May, With birds that carol, bees that hum—A

to our greeting   come: Come where music float-eth oft, On soft and balmy   air:
welcome, hap-py   day. Wild flowers now in fair - y nooks are shedding sweet per-fume, The

Ye whose hearts by grief are stirred, And ye whose skies are fair. }
Spring makes glad the mossy brooks, And all the meadows bloom. }   Tra la la la   la   la la

la   la la la la la la la, Tra la la la   la   la   la   la   la la la   la.

Sound our voices long and sweet, And roll the stirring drum; Friends and neighbors round us meet, And

to our greeting glad-ly come, To our greeting glad ly come, To our greeting come.

MUSIC IN SCHOOLS.—Controversy in reference to the introduction of the study of music in public schools is not uncommon. Those who oppose, hold that music is a specialty, that there is no general necessity for its culture, because its use is only for the few. A little observation will show the opposite of this to be the truth. What, indeed, is more common than music? It follows us from the cradle to the grave. The infant is cradled with a lullaby. Every ingleside blossoms with song. Every service of the sanctuary is strengthened by it. Every emotion of our human nature utters itself through it. Every convention is enlivened by it. Almost every town has its band, and every hamlet its instrument, and every hedge and grove their warblers. It is common almost as the air we breathe. The very fact of its use makes it useful, and shows its need. But it is said, How can a science so difficult and so hard

SWEET AND LOW.

Larghetto.

J. BARNBY.
ALFRED TENNYSON.

1. Sweet and low, sweet and low, Wind of the west - ern sea; Low, low, breathe and blow, Wind of the west - ern sea; O - ver the roll - ing wa - ters go, Come from the dy - ing moon and blow, Blow him a - gain to me, While my lit - tle one, while my pret - ty one sleeps..........

2. Sleep and rest, sleep and rest, Fa - ther will come to thee soon; Rest, rest on mother's breast, Fa - ther will come to thee soon; Fa - ther will come to his babe in the nest, Sil - ver sails all out of the west, Un - der the sil - ver moon Sleep, my lit - tle one, sleep, my pret - ty one, sleep..........

to master, be introduced into our common schools? No one expects the science to be mastered in the common schools. We have grammar; but who supposes that the common schools will exhaust the study, and send out accomplished philologists? We have reading and writing; but who supposes that the common schools are to turn out finished scholars in belles-lettres? What is desired is simply this,—that the presence and power of music shall be felt in the common schools. That the children shall be able to sing. That the teachers shall so far master the fundamental principles of the science, as to be able to guide the children in the culture of this department of art. The mother needs it in the family. Our manhood needs its refining and hallowing power. Our churches demand it. Our very nature by divine providence craves it, and no primary or secondary instruction can be complete without it.—*E. E. Higbee.*

LET OTHERS DREAM.

Spirited.

J. C. Johnson.

1. Let oth - ers dream of pleas-ant lands, Be-yond the stormy o - cean; Of gold - en treas-ure
2. 'Twas there in childhood's ear-ly day, I car-oled loud for glad-ness, And youth a - mid the

in the sand, And air in gen - tle mo - tion, There is a dear - er, hap - pier scene, To
ver-dant bowers, Had never thought of sad - ness. And now in sweet-est rev - e - rie, When

fan - cy oft ap - pear - ing, It is my na-tive val-ley's green, With beauty mild and cheering.
even-ing shades are fall-ing, Comes forth each pleasant memory, That time of light re - call - ing.

VESPER HYMN.

Moderato.

Bortnianski.
Thomas Moore.

1. Hark! the ves-per hymn is steal-ing O'er the wa - ters, soft and clear; Near-er yet and
2. Now like moonlight waves retreat-ing To the shore, it dies a - long; Now, like an - gry

near - er peal - ing, Soft it breaks up - on the ear, Ju - bi - la - te, Ju - bi - la - te,
surg - es meet - ing, Breaks the mingled tide of song. Ju - bi - la - te, Ju - bi - la - te,

f

Ju - bi - la - te, A* - men. Far-ther now, now farther stealing, Soft it fades up - on the ear.
Ju - bi - la - te, A - men. Hark! again, like waves retreating To the shore, it dies a - long.

p *rit*

* Pronounce as in *la* or *fa*-ther — II—B

RELIGION has yoked all the arts and sciences to her chariot, and one of the first of them was poetry, which expresses for us that to which logic and science cannot give utterance. Who does not thrill at the hymn of John Henry Newman, " Lead, Kindly Light," written when he felt the impending change of his whole life, that was to alienate him from so many friends and cast so much suspicion on him? Who does not feel the impulse of Bernard's " Jerusalem the Golden," or the *Veni, Creator*, written in the time of Charlemagne? Such hymns are outside of dogma; they are common to all churches, Catholic and Protestant. But you say these are too old for the Sunday-school. Perhaps they are, yet they are far better for such use than the doggerel verses so often employed. Hymns, if they must be simple, must also be dignified; it is absurd to set a great bearded fellow singing of his little hands and feet, of his fresh, clean face. It is no doubt necessary to teach children hymns they understand, but their future must be looked to; thus it is well to teach them hymns they

WHAT IS HOME WITHOUT A MOTHER?

ALICE HAWTHORNE.
Per. OLIVER DITSON & Co.

Moderato.

1. What is home with - out a mother? What are all the joys we meet,
2. Things we prize are first to van - ish, Hearts we love to pass a - way;
3. Old - er hearts may have their sor - rows, Griefs that quickly die a - way,

When her lov - ing smile no long - er Greets the coming, coming of our feet? The
And how soon, e'en in our childhood, We behold her turning, turn - ing grey: Her
But a moth - er lost in childhood Grieves the heart, the heart from day to day; We

days seem long, the nights are drear, And time rolls slow - ly on: And
eye grows dim, her step is slow; Her joys of earth are past; And
miss her kind, her will - ing hand, Her fond and ear - nest care; And

oh! how few are childhood's pleasures, When her gen - tle, gen - tle care is gone.
some - times 'ere we learn to know her, She hath breath'd on earth, on earth her last.
oh! how dark is life a - round us, What is home without, without her there.

do not wholly understand, that they may grow up with their ideas in them. Are not literary tastes formed in part by the selections in reading-books that we do not, as children, fully understand? Like the choice of these prose selections should be that of Sunday-school hymns; especially so should it be for those who are just about entering on manhood and womanhood. They should be given that which will be of greatest use to them.

HELEN sat down at the piano. Her time was perfect and she never blundered a note. She played well and woodenly, and had for her reward a certain wooden satisfaction in her own performance. The music she chose was good of its kind, but had more to do with the instrument than the feelings, was more dependent upon the execution than the expression. Bascombe yawned behind his handkerchief, and Wingfold gazed at the profile of the player, wondering how, with such fine features and complexion, with such a fine shaped and well-set head, her face should be so far short of interesting. It seemed a face that had no story.—*Macdonald.*

THAT SWEET STORY OF OLD.

GREEK MELODY.
JEMIMA THOMPSON-LUKE. 1841.

1. I think, when I read that sweet sto-ry of old, When Je-sus was here among men.
2. I wish that His hands had been placed on my head, That His arm had been thrown around me,
3. Yet still to His foot-stool in prayer I may go, And ask for a share in His love;
4. In that beau-ti-ful place He has gone to prepare For all who are washed and forgiv'n:

How He called lit-tle children as lambs to His fold, I should like to have been with them then.
And that I might have seen His kind look when He said, "Let the lit-tle ones come un-to Me."
And if I but earn-est-ly seek Him be-low, I shall see Him and hear Him a-bove,
And ma-ny dear chil-dren are gath-er-ing there, "For of such is the kingdom of heaven."

JOY BELLS RING TO-DAY.

SCOTCH AIR.

1. Joy bells ring through all the vale, Joy bells ring to-day; Bright the sun-ny
2. Dew-drops gleam up-on the grass, O-dors scent the air; Shad-ows from the
3. Sweet the lin-net's clear flute note, Nev-er life more fair; War-bling now each

Chorus.

hours we hail, 'Tis the hap-py May. Joy bells ring to-day, Through the vale a-
clouds that pass Make the scene more fair. Joy bells ring to-day, Through the vale a-
tune-ful throat; Vo-cal all the air. Joy bells ring to-day, Through the vale a-

far; Our gladness now there's nought to mar, The joy bells ring to-day.

Loiter we in childhood's dream, | Dreaming o'er our happy lot, | Mem'ry bells these sounds shall be,
  Fairy realms abound; | Heav'n ne'er seemed so near; | Tones that ne'er depart;
Linger we beside the stream, | Would you find Earth's favored | Mem'ry bells for thee and me,—
  Glory all around.—*Cho.* | Seek it, wand'rer, here. [spot. | We listen with the heart.—*Cho.*

MUSICAL TRASH.—I wish to express my unfeigned disgust at the flood of musical trash that is annually poured from our music publishing houses in the shape of new tune-books. Every fresh book must contain new and original music. The old tunes must be mangled past recognition, and the compiler must rack his brains to invent new and more dreadful abortions, labeled with astounding names, and called tunes. If all the organists in the country were to meet in convention, and then vote on the best and most useful chorals, they would blot out of existence nine-tenths of these tunes, and give us a list of not over one hundred congregational tunes of real merit. There are at least twenty-four hundred pages of new tunes published every year. Of these how many are worth the paper they are printed upon? Perhaps a dozen tunes. Taking all the civilized people in the world together, it is found that only one man in a million is a musical composer of real genius. Plenty of people can pick out a tune on the piano. They are not composers. We have in the United States a few men, like Zundel and Tuckerman, who can write a choral. The music they give us will live. As for the rest, to the trunk-maker with it! A poor tune-book will make good kindling. To the fire with the rubbish, and let the smoke rise as incense to pure art.—*Barnard.*

THE SUMMER DAYS ARE COMING.

Spirited.

CHAS. JEFFREYS

1. The sum-mer days are com-ing, The blos-soms deck the bough, The bees are gai-ly humming, And the birds are sing-ing now. We've had our May-day gar-lands, We have crown'd our May-day queen With a cor-o-net of ro-ses Set in leaves of bright-est green, But her reign is al-most o-ver, The spring is on the wane, Oh, haste thee, gen-tle Sum-mer, To our pleas-ant land a-gain.

2. The min-strel of the moon-light, The love-lorn night-in-gale, Hath sung his month of mu-sic, To the rose queen of the vale; And what though he be si-lent? As the night comes slowly on, We will trip a-long the green-sward To sweet mu-sic of our own. Oh, the sum-mer days are com-ing, And sum-mer nights more dear; Oh, haste thee, gen-tle Sum-mer, For there's joy when thou art near.

3. We'll rise and hail thee ear-ly, Be-fore the sun hath dried The dewdrops that will spar-kle On the green hedge by our side; And when the blaze of noonday Shines up-on the thirst-y flowers, We will seek the wel-come cov-ert Of our jas-mine shad-ed bowers. Oh, the sum-mer days are com-ing, The spring is on the wane; Oh, haste thee, gen-tle Sum-mer, To our pleas-ant land a-gain.

FLY AWAY, PRETTY MOTH.

Thos. H. Baily.

Allegretto.

1. Fly a - way, pret - ty Moth, to the shade   Of the   leaf where you slumber'd all
2. I have seen, pret - ty Moth, in the   world,   Some as   wild as yourself and as

day,   Be con - tent with the moon, and the   stars,   pret - ty Moth,   And make
gay,   Who, be - witch'd by the sweet   fas - ci - na - tion of eyes,   Flit - ted

use   of your wings while you   may.   Tho' yon glit - ter - ing light   May have
round them by night and by   day.   But though dreams   of de - light   May have

daz - zled you quite, Tho' the   gold   of yon lamp may be   gay,   Ma - ny
daz - zled them quite, They at   last found it dan - ger - ous   play!   Ma - ny

things in this world that look bright, pretty Moth, On - ly daz - zle to lead us a - stray;   Ma - ny
things in this world that look bright, pretty Moth, On - ly daz - zle to lead us a - stray;   Ma - ny

things in this world that look bright, pret - ty Moth, Only daz - zle to lead us a - stray.
things in this world that look bright, pret - ty Moth, Only daz - zle to lead us a - stray.

To Religion, music owes indeed a threefold homage. First, the earliest authentic records which we have in the history of music, as it now is, are records in the history of church music; so that music, as an art, began in the church. Second, the greatest workers in the realm of music, and a large majority of all the workers in that realm, have been earnest Christian men, influenced, and to a great extent controlled, by a strong religious zeal. Third, the subjects which have inspired the masterpieces of the classics, are themes taken from the Christian's guide-book, the Bible. Although the ancient Egyptians, Greeks and Romans had both vocal and instrumental music, yet, as Mr. Hunt says in his concise History of Music, "It is not until the fourth century after Christ, that the actual history of music as a separate art begins." Not only did it have its be-ginning in the Christian era, but it received its first tangible and permanent mold from zealous Christian men. They not only, as Choran says, "transmitted to us *all* the ancient practical music, with which we are acquainted," but they built upon this the foundation upon which the present superstructure stands. How long might music have languished and remained rude and uncultivated if there had not arisen such zealous Christian workers as Pope Sylvester, St. Ambrose, St. Gregory and Guido Aretina! The greatest composers of music, and those who have done most for the art, have been men of deep religious feeling, earnestly laboring to render their best service to a God whom they not only loved, but whom they believed to demand of them ten more talents for the talents he had lent. Under the influence of religious zeal a man will accom-

THE MILLER OF THE DEE.

Chas. Mackay.

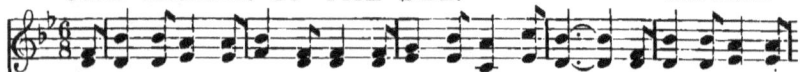

1. There dwelt a mil - ler, hale and bold, Be - side the riv - er Dee; He wrought and sang from morn till night, No lark more blithe than he; And this the bur - den of his song For ev - er used to be, "I en - vy no one—no, not I! And no one en - vies me!

2. "Thou'rt wrong, my friend!" said old king Hal, "As wrong as wrong can be; For could my heart be light as thine, I'd glad - ly change with thee. And tell me now what makes thee sing With voice so loud and free While I am sad, though I'm the King, Be - side the riv - er Dee?"

3. The mil - ler smiled and doffed his cap: "I earn my bread," quoth he; "I love my wife, I love my friend, I love my chil - dren three. I owe no one I can - not pay, I thank the riv - er Dee, That turns the mill that grinds the corn To feed my babes and me!"

4. "Good friend," said Hal, and sighed the while, "Farewell! and happy be; But say no more, if thou'dst be true, That no one en - vies thee; Thy mea - ly cap is worth my crown; Thy mill my kingdom's fee! Such men as thou are England's boast, Oh, mil - ler of the Dee!"

plish more than under any other impulse. Can we think of the author of "The Messiah" as any other than a religious man? Moore says, in his Encyclopedia, "Haydn was very religious; it may even be said that, through his firm faith in the truths of religion, his talent was increased." The commencement of all his scores was inscribed with some of the following mottoes: "In Nomine Domini," (In the name of the Lord) or "Soli Deo Gloria," (To God alone be glory) and, at the end of all of them, "Laus Deo." (Paise to God). He himself said: "When I was working on 'The Creation,' I felt myself so penetrated with religion, that, before I sat down to my piano, I prayed confidently to God to give me the talent requisite to praise him worthily." Of Mendelssohn, Lampadius says: "To speak out in a single word what was the most salient feature of his character, he was a Christian in the fullest sense." But, after all, the subject which the composer chooses, the theme, is often a fountain of inspiration. How could Haydn have written so grandly if he had not for a subject "The Creation?" What characters for grandeur are Elijah and St. Paul? What could have inspired Handel like "The Messiah," or upon what other theme could he have heard angelic hosts shouting "Hallelujah, hallelujah!" We need but mention such subjects as the Masses (for example, Beethoven's Mass in D), and the grandest and most sublime of all music, Bach's "Passion Music," "which will endure unto the end of time," to show what great, almost heavenly power, is drawn forth by religious subjects.—*More.*

BREATHINGS OF SPRING.

Von Weber.
Felicia Hemans.

Moderato. mf

Trio.

1. What wakest thou, Spring? sweet voices in the wood, And reed - like ech - oes that have long been mute, Thou bring - est back to fill the sol - i - tude, The lark's clear pipe, the cuc - koo's view - less flute, Whose tone seems breath-ing mournful - ness or glee, E'en as our hearts may be, our hearts may be, Whose tone seems breath - ing mourn ful-ness or glee, E'en as our hearts may be, E'en as our hearts may be.

2. And the leaves greet thee, Spring! the joy - ous leaves, Whose tremblings glad - den many a copse and glade, Whose each young spray a ro - sy flush re - ceives, When thy south wind hath pierced the cluster - ing shade, And hap - py mur - murs run-ning thro' the grass Tell that thy foot - steps pass, thy foot - steps pass, And hap - py mur - murs run-ning thro' the grass Tell that thy foot - steps pass, Tell that thy foot - steps pass.

3. And the bright wa - ters—they too hear thy call, Spring, the a - wak - ener! thou hast burst their sleep: A - midst the hol - lows of the rocks, their fall Makes mel - o - dy, and in the for - ests deep Where sud - den spark - les and blue gleams be - tray Their wind - ings to the day, windings to the day, Where sud - den spark - les and blue gleams be - tray Their windings to the day, Their wind - ings to the day.

4. And flow - ers! the fair-peopled world of flow - ers, Thou from the dust hast set that glo - ry free, Col - or - ing the cow-slips with the sunny hours, And pen - cil - ling the wood - an - e - mo - ne; Si - lent they seem yet each to po - e - sy, mute po - e - sy, Si - lent they seem, yet each to thoughtful eye, Glows with mute po - e - sy, Glows with mute po - e - sy.

THE OLD SONGS.—There are no songs like the old songs. In ancient times, that is to say, in the half-forgotten days of our youth, a species of song existed which exists no more. It was not as the mournful ballads of these days, which seem to record the gloomy utterances of a strange young woman who has wandered into the magic scene in "Der Frei-schutz," and who mixes up the moanings of her passion with descriptions of the sights and sounds she there finds around her. It was of quite another stamp. It dealt with a phraseology of sentiment peculiar to itself, a "patter," as it were, which came to be universally recognized in drawing rooms. It spoke of maidens plighting their troth, of Phillis enchanting her lover with her varied moods, of marble halls in which true love still remained the same. It apostrophized the shells of ocean; it tenderly described the crises of a particular heroine's life; it told of how the lover of pretty Jane would have her meet him in the evening. Well, all the world was

SILENCE! SILENCE!

ROETHEN.

1. Si-lence, si-lence, make no noise nor stir, Si-lence, si-lence, make no noise nor stir, For in yon bow-er there a-bove, Sleeps my gen-tle la-dy love; Si-lence, si-lence, make no noise nor stir, That in peace, that in peace, she may slum-ber sweet-ly on, That in peace, that in peace she sleep.

2. Si-lence, si-lence, make no noise nor stir, Si-lence, si-lence, make no noise nor stir, For na-ture lists with anx-ious ear, Her gentle slumb'ring breath to hear; Si-lence, si-lence, make no noise nor stir, Soft in peace, soft in peace, slumb-er, fair one, sweet-ly on, Soft in peace, soft in peace, sleep on.

3. Soft-ly, soft-ly, light-ly, gent-ly tread, Soft-ly, soft-ly, light-ly, gent-ly tread; And ere the break of wakening day, Soft-ly, light-ly, move a-way; Soft-ly, soft-ly, light-ly, gent-ly tread; Rest in peace, rest in peace, slumb'ring maid-en, love of mine, Rest in peace, rest in peace, fare-well.

content to accept this conventional phraseology, and, behind the paraphernalia of "enchanted moonbeams," and "fondest glances," and "adoring sighs," perceived and loved the sentiment that could find no simpler utterance. Some of us, hearing the half-forgotten songs again, suddenly forget the odd language, and the old pathos springs up again as fresh as in the days when our first love had just come home from boarding-school; while others, who have no old-standing acquaintance with these memorable songs, have somehow got attracted to them by the mere quaintness of their speech and simplicity of their airs.—*Black.*

OUR unconsciousness is no proof of the absence of sound. There are, doubtless, sounds in Nature of which we have no conception. Could our sense be quickened, what celestial harmony might thrill us! Professor Cooke beautifully says: "The very air around us may be resounding with the hallelujahs of the heavenly host, while our dull ears hear nothing but the feeble accents of our own broken prayers."

TWICKENHAM FERRY.

THEO. MARZIALS. CARL MATZ ARR.

Not too fast.

1. O - hoi - yeho, Hoyeho, Who's for the ferry? The briar's in the bud, and the sun's going down, And I'll
2. O - hoi - ye-ho, Hoyeho, "I'm for the ferry, The briar's in the bud, and the sun's going down, And it's
3. Ohoiyeho, Ho! you're too late for the ferry, The briar's in the bud, and the sun's going down, And he's

row ye so quick, and I'll row ye so steady, And 'tis but a penny to Twickenham town. The
late as it is, and I have-n't a penny, And how shall I get me to Twickenham town?" She'd
not rowing quick and he's not rowing steady, You'd think 'twas a journey to Twickenham town. "O -

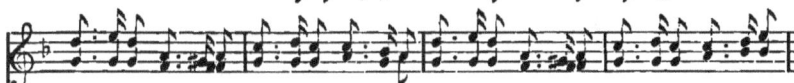

ferryman's slim and the ferryman's young, And he's just a soft twang in the turn of his tongue, And he's
a rose in her bonnet, and oh! she look'd sweet As the little pink flower that grows in the wheat, With her
hoi, and O - ho," you may call as you will, The moon is a-ris - ing   on   Petersham Hill, And with

fresh as a pip - pin and brown as a berry, And   'tis but a pen - ny to Twick - en - ham town.
cheeks like a rose and her lips like a cherry, "And sure and you're welcome to Twickenham town."
love like a rose in the stern of the wherry, There's danger in cross-ing to Twick - en - ham town.

Chorus.

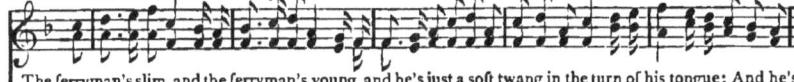

The ferryman's slim, and the ferryman's young, and he's just a soft twang in the turn of his tongue; And he's
[fresh as a pippin, and

CODA. After last verse. — *rall.*

brown as a berry, And 'tis but a penny to Twickenham town. Ohoiyeho, Hoyeho, Ho- ye-ho, Ho!

A SUFFICIENTLY accurate definition of music for our purpose is that it is "an agreeable succession of pleasing and harmonious sounds." Three essential elements enter into its composition—rhythm or accent, power, and tone; or measure, quantity, and quality. The first two seem to satisfy the untutored savage, whose tom-tom and Indian drum possess no other musical quality than a harsh sonorousness, whose monotony is only varied by the stronger or feebler beat given by the performer. As we rise in the scale of being from New Zealander to the man of culture and refinement, a Beethoven becomes not only a possibility, but a necessity; it is no greater stride from the barbaric death chant to the Seventh Symphony than from the infant stumbling over the alphabet to a Demosthenes or a Shakespeare. The influence of music in past ages and among by-gone peoples it is difficult now to estimate; but it has gone hand in hand with intellectual and æsthetic culture, and has ever been reckoned a divine art, an acknowledged force in moulding character and governing men. Radan relates a curious Hindoo legend celebrating the power of music: Men and animals move in harmony with the musician's wand, while all inanimate nature obeys the influence of music composed by the god Mahedo and his wife Parlutea. In the reign of Akbar a famous singer sang a "raga," consecrated to the night, in open day. Immediately the sun was eclipsed, and darkness spread as far as the voice was heard. There

ONCE AGAIN, O BLESSED TIME.

WM. BRIGHT.
ARTHUR SULLIVAN.

[*Christmas Hymn.*]

1. Once a-gain, O blessed time, Thankful hearts embrace thee: If we lost thy
2. Once a-gain the Ho-ly Night Breathes its blessing ten-der; Once a-gain the
3. Welcome Thou to souls a-thirst, Fount of end-less pleas-ure; Gates of hell may
4. Yea, if oth-ers stand a-part, We will press the near-er; Yea, O best fra-
5. So we yield Thee all we can, Wor-ship, thanks, and blessing; Thee true God, and

fes-tal chime, What could e'er re-place thee? Change will dark-en many a day,
Man-ger Light Sheds its gen-tle splen-dor; O could tongues by an-gels taught
do their worst, While we clasp our treas-ure; Wel-come, though an age like this
ter-nal Heart, We will hold Thee dear-er; Faith-ful lips shall an-swer thus
Thee true Man, On our knees con-fess-ing; While Thy birth-day morn we greet

Many a bond dis-sev-er; Many a joy shall pass a-way, But the "Great Joy" nev-er.
Speak our ex-ul-ta-tion, In the Virgin's Child that brought All man-kind sal-va-tion!
Puts Thy name on tri-al, And the truth that makes our bliss Pleads against de-ni-al.
To all faithless scorn-ing, "Je-sus Christ is God with us, Born on Christmas morn-ing.
With our best de-vo-tion, Bathe us, O most true and sweet! In Thy mercy's o-cean.

was another raga which burned him who dared to sing it. Akbar, desiring to make trial of it, ordered a musician to sing this song while plunged up to the neck in the sacred river of Jumna. In vain: the unfortunate singer became a prey to the flames. If these ancient legends convey no other lesson, they indicate a profound and wide-spread conviction of the power of music. Leaving an atmosphere that savors of fable, it is a matter of record that Alexander the Great was roused to fury by the Phrygian and calmed by the Lydian melodies of Timotheus. It is also related that an insurrection in Sparta was quelled by Terpander, who sang skillfully to the accompaniment of his harp. Our amusing Radan questions the wisdom, however, of arming the police of to-day with flutes and guitars as means of preserving the peace. We know what miracles of daring have been wrought by the proscribed volcanic "Marseillaise." Nor was the French general far wrong when he reported: "I have won the victory. The 'Marseillaise' commanded with me." Who shall say that Arndt's song, "What is the German Fatherland?" had not as much to do with the unification of his country as Bismarck's blood and iron? In our own land, in this day and generation, a Roman Catholic priest, who had been asked to explain the reason of the rapid and extraordinary spread of his religion, answered, with more frankness than reverence for dogma, "It is the blessing of God on good music."—*Gray.*

EDUCATION.—When a boy I was very fond of music, and am so now; and it so happened that I had the opportunity of hearing much good music. Among other things I had abundant opportunities of hearing that great old master, Sebastian Bach. I remember perfectly well—though I knew nothing about music then, and, I may add, know nothing whatever about it now—the intense satisfaction and delight which I had in listening by the hour together to Bach's fugues. It is a pleasure which remains with me, I am glad to think, but of late years I have tried to find out the why and wherefore, and it has often occurred to me that the pleasure in musical compositions of this kind is essentially of the same nature as that which is derived from pursuits which are commonly regarded as purely intellectual. I mean that the source of pleasure is exactly the same as in most of my problems in morphology—that you have the theme in one of the old master's works followed out in all its endless variations, always appearing and always reminding you of unity in variety. So in painting; what is called truth to nature is the intellectual element coming in, and truth to nature depends entirely upon the intellectual culture of the person to whom art is addressed. If you are in Australia, you may get the credit for being a good artist—I mean among the natives—if you can draw a kangaroo after a fashion. But among men of higher civilization the intellectual knowledge we possess brings its criticism into our appreciation of works of art, and we are obliged to satisfy it as well as the mere sense of beauty

COME, OH, COME WITH ME.

ITALIAN MELODY.

1. Come, O come with me, the moon is beam - ing, Come, O come with me; the stars are gleam - ing; All a - round, a - bove, with beau - ty teem - ing; Moon - light hours have joys for me. Tra la la la
2. My skiff is by the shore, she's light and free, To ply the feathered oar is joy to me; And while we glide a - long, o'er the dark blue sea, We'll sing our sweet - est mel - o - dy. Tra la la la

Ja la la la la la, Tra la la la la la la la la.

Fine. *D.C.*

in color and in outline. And so the higher the culture and information of those whom art addresses, the more exact and precise must be what we call its "truth to nature." If we turn to literature the same thing is true, and you find works of literature which may be said to be pure art. A little song of Shakespeare or of Goethe is pure art, although its intellectual content may be nothing. A series of pictures is made to pass before your minds by the meaning of words, and the effect is a melody of ideas. And if you will let me for a moment speak of the very highest forms of literature, do we not regard them as highest simply because the more we know the truer they seem, and the more competent we are to appreciate beauty the more beautiful they are? No man ever understands Shakespeare until he is old, though the youngest may admire him; the reason being that he satisfies the artistic instinct of the youngest and harmonizes with the ripest and richest experience of the oldest. It is not a question whether one order of study or another should predominate, but rather of what topics of education you shall select, combining all the needful elements in such due proportion as to give the greatest amount of food and support and encouragement to those faculties which enable us to appreciate truth, and to profit by those sources of innocent happiness which are open to us, and at the same time to avoid that which is bad and coarse and ugly, and to keep clear of the multitude of pitfalls and dangers which beset those who break through the natural or moral laws.—*Thos. H. Huxley.*

MILITARY MUSIC.—In the seventeenth century, we find the hautboy, an instrument of German origin, given to the dragoons and musketeers of the guard. We are indebted to the Hungarians, and through them to the eastern nations, for the kettledrum, the bassoon, and the true flute; for the tamborine to the Italians; the modern horn, to the Hanoverians; for the cymbals and big drum, to the Turks. The adoption of these last two instruments and the kettledrums, gave the name of Turkish music to certain military music. The combination of their instruments with the cavalry trumpet constituted, at the beginning of the eighteenth century, the entire musical scheme of the troops. Then each battalion, each company, had its particular and distinctive music. The drum, the fife, the horn, the bassoon, the big drum, and the cymbals belonged particularly to the infantry; the trumpet, the hautboy, the bagpipe, the kettledrum to the cavalry. An ordinance in France, in 1766, appointed a band of music to each regiment. It was composed of all the instruments which then belonged to the companies or sections of troops. The clarionet, invented in the beginning of the eighteenth century, by an inhabitant of Nuremburg, was not received into the military band of France before the year 1755. The serpent, invented in 1590, the triangle, which was the cymbal of the Middle Ages, and the trombone, entered successively into the different corps of the army. But it is only since 1792 that military music has been truly developed. Its utility has been

OLD FRIENDS AND OLD TIMES.

J. R. THOMAS.
Per. S. BRAINARD & SONS.

1. Thinking of old times, Hopes ne'er to be, Speaking of old friends, Far o'er the sea;
2. Oh, 'mid the old friends I no more see, Is there a kind thought Ever for me?

Solo.

Dis-tance can change not Dear ones like you; For-tunes estrange not Hearts that are true.
If there's but one hope, One wish though vain, If there's but one sigh, I'll not com-plain.

Duet.

Thus in the twi-light Fond thoughts will stray, Back to the old homes, Homes far a - way!
Thus in the twi-light Fond thoughts will stray, Thinking of old friends, Friends far a - way!

Chorus.

Homes far a - way, Far, far a - way, Homes far a - way, Far, far a - way.
Friends far a - way, Far, far a - way, Friends far a - way, Far, far a - way.

Far a - way, Far a - way,

a frequent theme of discussion. Who does not know the grand effect of a national air played by a military band previous to an engagement? The very coward is fired with enthusiasm by the strains of some home or national melody. There is no feeling implanted in man's nature, which so veritably deserves the name of instinct as a love of music. To the soldier, especially in time of war, it is grateful beyond measure. On his weary march, it takes from his fatigue; in distant climes it carries him back to his home; in the hour of battle it arouses ambition and incites to noble deeds of courage. Indeed, music is one of the most beneficial addenda to military improvement.—*Moore.*

THE proprietor of the Cyfarthfa iron works, Wales, organized among his men a brass band, which met for practice once a week, throughout the year. They numbered sixteen instruments. A visitor says, he heard them perform the overture to Zampa, the Caliph of Bagdad and Fra Diavolo, with a number of waltzes, polkas, etc. They took up the time well, and the instruments preserved it with spirit and accuracy. These men were in the mountains of Wales and had never listened to other bands. Their habits and manners, appeared to have been improved under the softening influence of music, which, from a doubtful and difficult experiment, had become a pleasant pastime.

MY AIN COUNTRIE.

M. A. Lee.

1. I am far frae my hame, an' I'm wea-ry aftenwhiles, For the lang'd-for hame-bringing, an' my
2. I've his gude word of promise, that some gladsome day the King To his ain roy-al pal-ace, his
3. He is faithfu' that hath promised, an' he'll surely come again, He'll keep his tryst wi' me, at what

Fa - ther's wel - come smiles, An' I'll ne'er be fu' con - tent un - -
ban - ished hame, will bring; Wi' een, an' wi' heart run - nin'
hour I din - na ken; But he bids me still to wait, an'

til my een do see The gowd - en gates of heav'n, an' my ain coun-trie.
owre we shall see "The King in his beau-ty," an' our ain coun-trie.
read - y aye to be, To gang at on - y mo-ment to my ain coun-trie.

The earth is fleck'd wi' flow - ers, mon - y - tint - ed, fresh, and gay;
My sins hae been mon - y, and my sor - rows hae been sair;
So I'm watch-ing aye, and singing o' my hame as I wait,

The bird - ies war - ble blithely, for my Fa-ther made them sae; But these
But there they'll nev - er vex me, nor be re - mem - bered mair. For his
For the soun'- ing o' his foot-fa' this side the gowd - en gate, God gie his

sichts an' these soun's will as naething be to me, When I hear the angels singing in my ain countrie.
bluid hath made me white, and his hand shall dry my e'e, When he brings me hame at last to my ain countrie.
grace to ilk ane wha lis-tens noo to me, That we a' may gang in gladness to our ain countrie.

MECHANICAL MUSIC.—The Black Forest is famous for these mechanical organs—orchestrions, as they are called—and in some instances they are brought to great perfection. There is a shop close to the exhibition, bearing the name of Lamy Söhne, full of clocks and singing-birds and orchestrions, where you may pass half an hour in a fairy-land of surprises and all kinds of mechanical music. One morning I went in with an old lady and gentleman—the latter a grave dignitary of the church of England. "A very tiring place," said the old lady; "all up and down hill; the only fault I find with the Black Forest. Couldn't they level it, my dear?"—to her husband—"or build viaducts or something? Or, at the very least, couldn't they organize pony chaises all over the country—like those, you know, that we found so useful at Bournemouth last year? "Take a chair, my love," said the old gentleman sympathetically, without committing himself to an opinion. And he placed one for her, while the young man in the shop (whose jolly, good-natured face and broad grin delighted one to behold) wound up the orchestrion. The old lady sat down somewhat heavily from sheer exhaustion, and immediately the chair struck

HEARTS AND HOMES.

J. BLOCKLEY.

1. Hearts and homes, sweet words of pleas-ure, Mus - ic breath - ing as ye fall; Mak - ing
2. Hearts and homes, sweet words re - veal-ing, All most good and fair to see; Fit - ting

each the oth - er's trea - sure, Once di - vid - ed, los - ing all. Homes, ye
shrines for pur - est feel - ing, Tem - ples meet to bend the knee. In - fant

may be high or low - ly, Hearts a - lone can make you ho - ly; Be the
hands bright gar - lands wreathing, Hap - py voi - ces in - cense breathing, Em - blems

dwell - ing e'er so small, Hav - ing love, it boast - eth all.
fair of realms a - bove, For love is heav'n, and heav'n is love.

up the lively air of "The Watch on the Rhine," with a decidedly martial influence upon its occupant. She sprang from her seat as if it had been a gridiron, and asked her husband reproachfully if he was amusing himself at her expense, and whether her age was not sufficient to secure her from practical joking. "Dear me!" cried he, in amazement, looking at the offending chair as though he expected it to walk away of its own accord. "What a musical nation these Black Foresters are! It's music everywhere! The very chairs you sit down upon are full of it." At this moment the orchestrion struck up an operatic selection, and the old lady recovered her amiability in listening to a really fine instrument. I left them marveling at all the birds and boxes, and thinking each as it came more wonderful than the last.—*Argosy.*

THE influence of music on the young, the ignorant and depraved is not perhaps sufficiently regarded. Watch the crowd that collects around the street organist. His first note is the signal for all hastily to assemble. The care-worn and furrowed cheek is at once lighted up with a pleasant smile. The beggar forgets his penury, the laborer his toil, the boy with satchel at his back, forgets the hour for school. The tear in the nursery is quickly followed by a bright and joyous smile, as Biddy hastens with her charge to the door.

THE ROSY CROWN.

C. M. VON WEBER.
Words by D. DUTTON.

1. A ro - sy crown we twine for thee, Of Flo - ra's rich - est treas - ure, We
2. The myr - tle, thyme, and eg - lan - tine, One blend - ed wreath dis - clo - ses; And

lead thee forth to dance and glee, To mirth and youthful pleas ure.
bid their frangrant breath combine With these em-blushing ro - ses.

Take, O take the

ro - sy, the ro- sy crown, Take, O take the ro - sy, the ro - sy crown.

3. We bade the fairest flowers that grow,
Their varied tribute render,
To shine above that brow of snow,
In all their sunny splendor.
Take, O take, etc.

4. Then deign to wear the wreath we twine,
Thy beauteous ringlets shading;
And be its charms a type of thine,
In all except their fading.
Take, O take, etc.

THREE CHILDREN SLIDING.

A. D. 1633.

mf

Not too Fast.

1. Three child - ren slid - ing on the ice, All on a sum - mer's day, As
2. Now had these chil - dren been at home, Or slid - ing on dry ground, Ten
3. You pa - rents all that chil - dren have, And you, too, that have none, If

rit.

it fell out they all fell in, The rest they ran a - way.
thous - and pounds to pen - ny one, They had not all been drown'd:
you would have them safe a - broad, Pray keep them safe at home.

* Grace notes In Chorus are the original music in opera of "Der Freischutz," from which this is taken.

NURSERY RHYMES.—Many of these productions have a very curious history, but cannot always be fully traced. Some of them probably owe their origin to names distinguished in our literature; as Oliver Goldsmith, for instance, is believed in his earlier days to have written such compositions. Dr. E. F. Rimbault gives us the following particulars as to some well-known favorites: "Sing a Song of Sixpence" is as old as the sixteenth century. "Three Blind Mice" is found in a music-book dated 1609. "The Frog and the Mouse" was licensed in 1580. "Three Children Sliding on the Ice" dates from 1633. "London Bridge is Broken Down" is of unfathomed antiquity. "Girls and Boys, Come out to Play" is certainly as old as the reign of Charles II.; as is also "Lucy Locket lost her Pocket," to the tune of which the American song of "Yankee Doodle" was written. · Pussy Cat, Pussy Cat, where have you been?" is of the age of Queen Bess. "Little Jonny Horner" is older than the seventeenth century. "The Old Woman Tossed in a Blanket" is of the reign of James II., to whom it is supposed to allude.

WESLEY saw a difference between loud talking and screaming. To a screamer he once said: "Scream no more at the peril of your soul. God now warns you by me, whom he has set over you. Speak as earnestly as you can, but do not scream. Speak with all your heart, but with a moderate voice. It was said of our Lord, 'He shall not cry;' the word properly translated means, 'He shall not scream.'"

BRIGHTLY.

Allegretto.　　　　From HAYDN'S "SEASONS."

1. Bright - ly, bright - ly gleam the sparkling rills; Sum - mer, sum - mer
2. O - dors, o - dors load the sum - mer air, Mus - ic, mus - ic
3. Faint - ly, faint - ly sounds the dis - tant fall; Light - ly, light - ly

Semi-Chorus.

sleeps on ver - dant hills, A - mid the shades we ram - bling stray, Where cooling fountains
sweet - ly ech - oes there; And bright-est maids, with soft - est glance, Then join the song and
wood - land ech - oes call, And in their voice we seem to hear The tones of friends once

Chorus.

sport - ive play.
lead the dance.　Peal - ing, peal - ing come the laugh and shout; While
gay and dear.

gai - ly we sing till the old for - ests ring, While gai - ly we sing till the

old for-ests ring With the joy of our mer - ry rout, With the joy of our mer - ry rout.

ANGELS EVER BRIGHT AND FAIR.

Slowly.

HANDEL.

An - gels ev - er bright and fair, An - gels ev - er bright and fair, Take, O take me, Take, O

take me to your care, Take, O take me, Take, O take me to your care, An - gels

ev - er bright and fair, Take, O take me to your care, Take, O take me to your care.

GOLDEN SLUMBERS KISS YOUR EYES.

Smoothly.

LULLABY OF 17TH CENTURY.

1. Gold - en slum - bers kiss your eyes, Smiles a - wake you when you rise;
2. Care is heav - y, there - fore sleep; You are care, and care must keep;

Sleep, pret - ty loved ones, do not cry, And I will sing a lul - la - by,
Sleep, pret - ty loved ones, do not cry, And I will sing a lul - la - by,

Lul - la - by, lul - la - by, lul - la - by.

11—C

THE introduction of music into the public schools is a step in the right direction. If in every town and village in the Union the plan was as faithfully and earnestly executed as in Boston and its vicinity, already the great work would be almost accomplished. We need fresh impetus in every country town, in every village nestled among the hills or stretching out on the wide prairies. There is surely in every such place some earnest disciple who could gather a band of ten or a dozen who should be a nucleus for a musical association. The influence of musical culture which would result from such an association would make itself felt through the village church as well as in social relations; Sunday service would be better, and the best part of Sunday service would get into the week-days. It will not do to make the gathering merely a psalm-singing school; that has its use and has its day of separate influence. Sacred music, so called, should form a part of the practical programme; but a little care and research,

ROLL ON, SILVER MOON.

J. W. TURNER.

Andante.

1. As I stray'd from my cot at the close of the day, 'Mid the ravishing beauties of June, 'Neath a
2. As the hart on the mountain my lov-er was brave, So no-ble and manly and clev-er, So
3. But, a - las! he is dead, and gone to death's bed, — Cut down like a rose in full bloom; And a -
4. His lone grave I'll seek out until morning appears, And weep o'er my lover so dear; I'll em-
5. Ah, me! ne'er a-gain may my bosom rejoice, For my lost love I fain would meet soon; And fond

jes - sa-mine shade I es - pied a fair maid, And she plain-tive-ly sighed to the moon..
kind and sin - cere, and he loved me full dear, Oh, my Edwin, his e - qual was nev-er!''
lone doth he sleep, while I thus sad-ly weep 'Neath thy soft sil - ver light, gen-tle moon.
brace the cold sod, and bathe with my tears, The sweet flow - ers that bloom o'er his grave.
lov - ers will weep o'er the grave where we sleep, 'Neath thy soft sil - ver light, gen-tle moon.

Roll on, sil - ver moon, guide the trav'ler his way, While the nightingale's song is in tune; I

cres. f   dim.

nev - er, nev - er-more with my true love will stray By thy soft sil - ver beams, gentle moon.

a correspondence with some musical authority in our large cities, would insure a judicious selection of attractive music within the compass of choirs and choruses of even very moderate ability. The modifying influence in a country town of a musical association conducted on broad, liberal principles for even a single decade, is incalculable. Polybius was a wise man in remarking that in Arcadia, a dull, cold country, music was essential to soften the manners of the inhabitants, and that in Cynetus, where music was not cultivated, vice prevailed to an alarming extent. Music will not hold its true place till, through the length and breadth of the land, it is recognized as elevating in its character, capable of perversion and misuse—as God's own word may be in the hands of the blasphemer—but a power still, infinite in truth and beauty, and a source of strength, encouragement, and inspiration to waiting thousands.

IN THE STARLIGHT.

STEPHEN GLOVER.
J. E. CARPENTER. C. MATZ Arr.

1. In the starlight, in the star-light, let us wan-der gay and free, For there's nothing in the
2. In the starlight, in the star-light, at the day-light's dew-y close, When the nightin-gale is

day-light half so dear to you and me.   Like the fai-ries in the shad-ow   of the
sing-ing his last love-song to   the rose;   In the calm clear night of summer, when the

dim.

woods we'll steal a - long,   And our sweetest lays we'll war-ble, for the night was made for
breez-es soft-ly   play,   From the glit-ter of our dwell-ing we will gen-tly   steal a-

rit.   *a tempo.*   *cres.*

song;   When none are by to lis-ten, or to chide us   in   our glee, In the
way   Where the silv'ry wa-ters mur-mur, by the mar-gin   of   the sea, In the

star-light, in the starlight, let us wander   gay and free,   In the starlight, in the starlight, let us
star-light, in the starlight, we will wander   gay and free,   In the starlight, in the starlight, we will

cres.   *a tempo*

wan-der, let us wan-der, In the star-light,   in the star-light, let us wander gay and free.
wan-der, we will wander, In the star-light,   in the star-light, we will wander gay and free.

WHENEVER a strike of dissatisfied workmen occurs in any city of France, the strikers give expression to their feelings by marching through the streets singing the Marseillaise. Whenever an individual in any part of France, suffers wrong at the hand of a judge or other public functionary, he takes revenge in singing, or attempting to sing the Marseillaise. When the students of a school in Paris quarrel with their professor, they drive him from his chair as they sing the Marseillaise. In short, whenever a Frenchman anywhere in France is subjected to any indignity or outrage, or feels discontented, or gets highly excited, he betakes himself to the public highway or private apartment, where he sings, or thinks about singing, the Marseillaise. It is a happy thing for Frenchmen that they have such a stirring national hymn as the Marseillaise.

WE HAVE LIVED AND LOVED TOGETHER.

NICOLO.
CHARLES JEFFREYS.

Andantino.

1. We have lived and loved together Thro' many changing years, We have shared each other's gladness, And wept each other's tears. I have never known a sorrow That was long unsooth'd by thee, That was long unsooth'd by thee, For thy smile can make a summer Where darkness else would be, For thy smile can make a summer, Where darkness else would be.

2. Like the leaves that fall around us, In Autumn's fading hours; And the traitor smiles that darken, When the cloud of sorrow lowers, And tho' many such we've known, love, Too prone alas! to range, Too prone alas! to range, We both can speak of one, love, Whom time could never change, We both can speak of one, love, Whom time could never change.

3. We have lived and loved together Thro' many changing years, We have shared each other's gladness, And wept each other's tears. And let us hope, the future, As the past has been, will be, As the past has been, will be; I will share with thee thy sorrows, And thou thy joys with me, I will share with thee thy sorrows, And thou thy joys with me.

Ral - len - tan - do.

STARS TREMBLING O'ER US.

Andante.

D. M. MULOCH.

1. Stars trembling o'er us, And sun-set before us, Moun-tain in shadow and
2. Come not, pale Sor-row, Flee, flee till to-mor-row, Rest soft-ly fall-ing o'er
3. As the waves cov-er The depths we glide o-ver, So let the past in for-
4. Heav'n shines a-bove us, Bless all that love us,— All that we love, in thy

for-est a sleep,
eye-lids that weep; } Down the dim riv-er We float on for-ev-er, Speak not, ah,
get-ful-ness sleep,
ten-der-ness keep,

breathe not! there's peace on the deep, Speak not, ah, breathe not! there's peace on the deep.

rit.

BIRDS ARE IN THE WOODLAND.

KINDERGARTEN.

1. Birds are in the wood-land, birds are on the tree, Mer-ry Spring is com-ing,
2. Fruits are ripe in Au-tumn, leaves are sere and red, Then we glean the corn-fields,

glad of heart are we, Then come sport-ive breez-es, fields with flow'rs are gay,
thank-ing God for bread, Then at last comes Win-ter, fields are cold and lorn,

In the woods we're singing, thro' the Summer day, In the woods we're singing, thro' the Summer day.
But there's happy Christmas, when our Lord was born, Then there's happy Christmas, when our Lord was [born.

EARLY GENIUS.—Gounod, the musical composer, early manifested his talent. How he secured liberty to follow the bent of his genius, is told in the following incident: It seems that when a boy at college, every effort was made to destroy his musical genius. His professor, M. Poirson, was in despair. His parents intended him for the *ecole normale*. On its being announced to him that he was to go up for the necessary examination, the boy burst into tears, and steadily refused to continue his classical studies. His mother appealed to M. Poirson, and implored him to recall her boy to what she considered to be his duty. The stern professor accordingly sent for him, and, in a tone more threatening than encouraging, said to him: "So you wish to be a musician?" "Yes, sir," replied the terrified boy. "But that is not a profession." "What, sir; the profession of Beethoven, of Mozart, of Gluck, is not a profession?" "But, remember that Mozart at your age had composed music worth publishing, whereas you have only scribbled notes on paper. However, here is your last chance; if you really are a musician, you can set words to music." The old man copied out the poem, "Joseph," "A peine au sortir de l'en France." The boy hurried to his school desk, and after studying the subject, wrote an air and accompaniment, which he brought

MARY OF ARGYLE.

S. NELSON.

Moderato.

1. I have heard the mavis singing His love-song to the morn; I have seen the dew-drops clinging To the rose just new-ly born; But a sweeter song has cheer'd me At the evening's gentle close, And I've seen an eye still brighter Than the dew-drop on the rose; 'Twas thy voice, my gentle Mary, And thine art-less, winning smile, That made this world an E - den, Bon-ny Ma-ry of Ar-gyle.

2. Though thy voice may lose its sweetness, And thine eye its brightness, too, Though thy step may lack its fleetness, And thy hair its sun-ny hue, Still to me wilt thou be dearer Than all the world shall own; I have loved thee for thy beauty, But not for that a - lone. I have watch'd thy heart, dear Mary, And its goodness was the wile That has made thee mine forever, Bon-ny Ma-ry of Ar-gyle.

back to his professor, and showed to him, pale with emotion. He felt that on his judgment his future career depended. He sang it to the old man, who listened in amazement, and led him to his drawing room, where he made him play the accompaniment on a piano. Those present were enraptured by the beauty of the composition, and it was at once decided that young Gounod must follow the bent of the undoubted genius with which he was gifted.

THAT we may sympathize truly, we must in a degree partake of the feelings of others; and this can only be done in proportion to their truthful and delicate delineation. Whatever aids in that aids in promoting happiness, and, as the feelings become more worthy of expression, so every means of expressing them should become more eagerly welcomed. There is no doubt that the effects of good music upon the feelings themselves are most beneficial, allaying evil passions, calming undue excitement, soothing sorrow, and inspiring fresh hope and courage in the despondent. If it be found also to have the power of developing the language by which heart speaks to heart, and thus of drawing humanity nearer together in sympathy, an additional reason will arise for its cultivation, and the delight which it now affords will be but a foretaste of the richer and deeper happiness it has in store for us.

KILLARNEY.

M. W. BALFE'S LAST SONG.

Moderato.

1. By Kil-lar - ney's lakes and fells, Em'-rald isles and wind-ing bays, Mountain paths and
2. In - nis-fal - len's ruin - ed shrine May suggest a pass-ing sigh; But man's faith can
3. No place else can charm the eye With such bright and va - ried tints, Ev' - ry rock that
4. Mu - sic there for e - cho dwells, Makes each sound a har - mo - ny; Ma - ny-voiced the

woodland dells, Mem-'ry ev - er fond - ly strays, Boun-teous na-ture loves all lands,
ne'er de - cline Such God's wond - ers float - ing by; Cas - tle Lough and Glena bay;
you pass by, Ver-dure broid - ers or besprints, Vir - gin there the green grass grows,
cho - rus swells, 'Till it faints in ec - sta-sy. With the charmful tints be - low,

Beau - ty wan - ders ev - 'ry where, Foot-prints leaves on ma - ny strands,
Moun - tains Tore and Ea - gle's Nest; Still at Mu - cross you must pray
Ev - 'ry morn springs na - tal day, Bright-hued ber - ries daff the snows,
Seems the heav'n a - bove to vie, All rich col ors that we know,

rall. *dim.* 𝆏𝆏 *a tempo.*

But her home is sure - ly there! An - gels fold their wings and rest, In that E den
Tho' the monks are now at rest. An - gels won - der not that man There would fain pro-
Smil - ing win - ter's frown a - way. An - gels oft en pausing there, Doubt if E - den
Tinge the cloud-wreaths in that sky. Wings of an - gels so might shine, Glancing back soft

cres. *f*

of the West, Beau - ty's home, Kil - lar - - ney, Ev - er fair Kil - lar - ney.
long life's span, Beau - ty's home, Kil - lar - - ney, Ev - er fair Kil - lar - ney.
were more fair, Beau - ty's home, Kil - lar - - ney, Ev - er fair Kil - lar - ney.
light di - vine, Beau - ty's home, Kil - lar - - ney, Ev - er fair Kil - lar - ney.

SOUNDS.—We are all so accustomed to trust to our sight to guide us in most of our actions, and to think of things as we see them, that we often forget how very much we owe to sound. And yet nature speaks to us so much by her gentle, her touching, or her awful sounds, that the life of a deaf person may be even more hard to bear than that of a blind one. Have you ever amused yourself with trying how many different sounds you can distinguish if you listen at an open window in a busy street? You will probably be able to recognize easily the jolting of the heavy wagon or dray, the rumble of the omnibus, the smooth roll of the private carriage, and the rattle of the light butcher's cart; and even while you are listening for these, the crack of the carter's whip, the cry of the costermonger at his stall, and the voices of the passers-by will strike upon your ear. Then, if you give still more close attention, you will hear the doors open and shut along the street, the footsteps of the passengers, the scraping of the shovel of the mud-carts; nay, if he happen to stand near, you may even hear the jingling of the shoeblack's pence as he plays pitch and toss upon the pavement. If you think for a moment, does it not seem wonderful that you should hear all these sounds so that you can recognize each one distinctly while all the rest are

OLD GRIMES.

ALBERT G. GREENE.

1. Old Grimes is dead, that good old man, We ne'er shall see him more; He wore a sin-gle-
2. When-e'er was heard the voice of pain, His breast with pi-ty burned; The large, round head up-
3. He lived at peace with all mankind, In friendship he was true; His coat had pock-et-

breast-ed coat, That buttoned down be-fore. His heart was op-en as the day, His
on his cane, From i-vo-ry was turned. Thus ev-er prompt at pi-ty's call, He
holes be-hind, His pan-ta-loons were blue, But poor old Grimes is now at rest, Nor

feel-ings all were true; His hair it was in-clined to grey, He wore it in a queue.
knew no base de-sign; His eyes were dark, and rath-er small, His nose was a-qui-line.
fears misfortune's frown; He had a dou-ble-breast-ed vest, The stripes ran up and down.

4. He modest merit sought to find,
    And pay it its desert;
  He had no malice in his mind,
    No ruffle on his shirt.
  His neighbors he did not abuse,
    Was sociable and gay;
  He wore not rights and lefts for shoes,
    But changed them every day.

5. His knowledge, hid from public gaze,
    He never brought to view;
  He made a noise town-meeting days,
    As many people do.
  Thus, undisturbed by anxious care,
    His peaceful moments ran;
  And everybody said he was
    A fine old gentleman.

going on around you? But suppose you go into the quiet country. Surely there will be silence there. Try some day and prove it for yourself; lie down on the grass in a sheltered nook and listen attentively. If there be ever so little wind stirring you will hear it rustling gently through the trees; or even if there is not this, it will be strange if you do not hear some wandering gnat buzzing, or some busy bee humming as it moves from flower to flower. Then a grass-hopper will set up a chirp within a few yards of you, or, if all living creatures are silent, a brook not far off may be flowing along with a rippling, musical sound. These and a hundred other noises you will hear in the most quiet country spot; the lowing of cattle, the song of the birds, the squeak of the field-mouse, the croak of the frog, mingling with the sound of the woodman's axe in the distance, or the dash of some river torrent. And besides these quiet sounds, there are still other occasional voices of nature which speak to us from time to time. The howling of the tempestuous wind abroad in its fury, the roaring of the sea-waves in a storm, the crash of thunder and its reverberations among the hills, and the mighty noise of the falling avalanche; such sounds as these tell us how great and how terrible nature can be in her varied moods.—*Buckley.*

HOE OUT YOUR ROW.

Arr. from DONIZETTI.

Allegretto.

1. One sul - try day a farm-er's boy Was hoe-ing in the field of corn, And
2. Al-though a hard one was the row, And farm-ers paid but mea-gre hire, The
3. The lad the text re - mem-ber'd long, And oft - en proved the mor-al well, That

anx-ious-ly had wait-ed long To hear the wel-come din-ner horn; The
lad had work'd from ear-ly morn, And now be-gin-ning well to tire—"I
per-se-ver-ance to the end, At last will al-ways no-bly tell, Take

wel-come call was heard at last, And down he quick-ly dropp'd his hoe; The
can," said he, and man-ful-ly He seized a-gain his fall-en hoe; The
cour-age, then, re-solve you can, And strike an earn-est, vig'r-ous blow; In

farm-er shout-ed in his ear, "Hoe out your row! hoe out your row!"
good man pleased, now smiled to see The farm-er's boy hoe out his row.
life's great field of va-ried toil, Hoe out your row, hoe out your row!

TIME DOTH PASS AWAY.

"SCHOOL DAYS."

1. Ga-ther ro-ses while they bloom, Nev-er lose a day, Nor in sloth one hour con-
2. Now you've op-por-tu-ni-ty, Both for work and play; Where may you to-mor-row
3. Men have mourned their whole life through One good deed's delay; Do at once what you've to

sume, Time doth pass a-way, Nor in sloth one hour con-sume, Time doth pass a-way.
be? Time doth pass a-way, Where may you to-mor-row be? Time doth pass a-way.
do, Time doth pass a-way, Do at once what you've to do, Time doth pass a-way.

HOW SOFTLY ARE GLANCING.

MOZART.
FROM "MAGIC FLUTE."

p Solo.

Allegretto.

La, la, la, la, la, la, la, la, la, la, la, la, la, la, la, la, la, la, la,

la, la, la, la, la, la, la, la, la, la, la, la, la, la, la,

pp Chorus.

How soft-ly are glanc-ing Bright stars on the tide, Tra, la, la, la, la,
Then, bend-ing with vig-or, We ply the light oar, Tra, la, la, la, la,

pp

la, la, la, tra, la, la, la, la, As on the waves dancing in si-lence we
la, la, la, tra, la, la, la, la, We sing as we row till we're near-ing the

Fine.

glide, Tra, la, la, la, la, la, la, la, la, la, la, la, la.
shore, Tra, la, la, la, la, la, la, la, la, la, la, la, la.

Sooth-ing balm for ev-'ry smart This sweet music car - ries, And in ev-'ry
Where such love-ly songs a-bound Whose sweet echo press - es With a clear and

p   *f*

hu - man heart Soft e - mo - tion tar - ries. Then a - way with grief and pain,
joy - ous sound To the heart's re - cess - es, We would ev - er live in peace,

With us now shall mus - ic reign! In this vale shall mus - ic, sweet mus - ic
Har - mo - ny would nev - er cease. Har - mo - ny would nev - er, would nev - er

p

reign! O there are too man - y tears, Then with cheer - ful voi - ces
cease. Con - cord, friendship, peace a - lone Can our bur - dens light - en,

p

D.C.

Let us fill the liv - ing years Till the world re - joi - ces.
Then first sounds con - tent - ment's tone, Life on earth to bright - en.

THE ECHO.

m   *f*

1. O hark! O hear! How soft and clear The ech - o's mel - low strain! O
2. The gen - tle breeze A - mong the trees The ech - o wafts a - long; We
3. The mu - sic floats In soft - est notes Up - on the zeph - yr's wing; O

pp   *f*   *pp*

ech - o, hear! O ech - o, hear! Re - ply a - gain, a - gain, a - gain, a - gain.
call a - gain, We call a - gain, O hear our song, our song, our song, our song.
hear the song! O hear the song! A - gain we sing, we sing, we sing, we sing.

MERE NOISE.—Why do we not hear all sounds as music? Why are some mere noise, and others clear musical notes? This depends entirely upon whether the sound-waves come quickly and regularly, or by an irregular succession of shocks. For example, when a load of stones is being shot out of a cart, you hear only a long, continuous noise, because the stones fall irregularly, some quicker, some slower, here a number together, and there two or three stragglers by themselves; each of these different shocks comes to your ear and makes a confused, noisy sound. But if you run a stick very quickly along a paling, you will hear a sound very like a musical note. This is because the rods of the paling are all at equal distances one from the other, and so the shocks fall quickly one after another at regular intervals upon your ear. Any quick and *regular* succession of sounds makes a note, even though it may be a disagreeable one. The squeak of a slate pencil along a slate, and the shriek of a railway whistle are not pleasant, but they are real notes similar to those which can be produced on a violin.

THE CUCKOO.

1. Now the sun is in the west, Sink-ing slow behind the trees, And the Cuckoo, welcome guest,
2. Cheerful see yon shepherd boy, Climbing up the crag-gy rocks, As he views the dappled sky,

Gent-ly woos the even-ing breeze, Cuckoo! Cuckoo! Cuckoo! Cuckoo! Gently woos the
Pleas'd the Cuckoo's note he mocks, Cuckoo! Cuckoo! Cuckoo! Cuckoo! Pleas'd the Cuckoo's

evening breeze. Sportive now the swallows play, Lightly skimming o'er the brook, Darting swift they
note he mocks. Now advancing o'er the plain, Evening's dusky shades appear, And the Cuckoo's

wing their way, Homeward to their peaceful nook, Whilst the Cuckoo, bird of Spring, Still amidst the
voice a - gain Soft - ly steals up - on mine ear. While re-tir - ing from the view, Thus she bids the

trees doth sing, Cuckoo! Cuckoo! Cuckoo! Cuckoo! Still amidst the trees doth sing.
day a - dieu, Cuckoo! Cuckoo! Cuckoo! Cuckoo! Thus she bids the day a - dieu.

SPRING, GENTLE SPRING.

J. RIVIÈRE.
J. R. PLANCHÉ.

1. Spring! Spring! gen - tle Spring! Young - est sea - son of the year, Hith - er
2. Spring! Spring! gen - tle Spring! Gust - y March be - fore thee flies, Gloom - y

haste, and with thee bring A - pril with her smile and tear; Hand in hand with
Win - ter ban - ish - ing; Clear - ing for thy path the skies. Flocks and herds, and

joc - und May, Bent on keep - ing ho - li - day. With thy dai - sy di - a -
meads and bow'rs, For thy gra - cious pres - ence long! Come and fill the fields with

dem, And thy robe of bright - est green,— We will wel - come thee and them,
flow'rs, Come and fill the woods with song.— We will wel - come thee and them,

As ye've ev - er welcomed been. Spring! Spring! gen - tle Spring! Young - est sea - son

of the year, Life and joy to na - ture bring! Na - ture's dar - ling, haste thee here.

THE incident which gave rise to the song, "True Love Can Ne'er Forget," by Samuel Lover, has been the foundation of several other ballads, some of them translated from the ancient Irish. The story runs that Carolan, a blind harper, recognized his early love, Bridget Cruise, by the touch of her hand, although he had not met her for twenty years. The old lover was playing by the water, when a ferry-boat drew near, and he chanced to assist the lady to alight. Turlogh O'Carolan, the bard, was one of the characters of Ireland. He was born in Nobber, county Westmeath, in 1670, and was the last of the ancient race of Irish bards. He lost his eyesight at the age of sixteen. He made very beautiful words, but was chiefly noted for his exquisite melodies. Goldsmith, who had seen him in his boyhood, wrote in later life: "His songs may be compared to those of Pindar, they bearing the same flight of imagination."—*Familiar Songs.*

TRUE LOVE CAN NE'ER FORGET.

SAMUEL LOVER.

1. "True love can ne'er for-get, Fond-ly as when we met, Dear-est, I love thee yet,
2. "Long years are past and o'er, Since from this fa-tal shore, Cold hearts and cold winds bore
3. Where minstrel sat a-lone, That la-dy fair hath gone; In his hand she placed her own—

Fine.

My dar-ling one!" Thus sang a min-strel gray, His sweet im-pas-sioned lay,
My love from me." Scarce-ly the min-strel spoke, When forth with flash-ing stroke,
He bowed his knee. With lips whence blessings came, He kissed with tru-est flame

Down by the o-cean's spray, At set of sun. With-ered was the min-strel's sight,
Light oars the si-lence broke O-ver the sea, Soon up-on her na-tive strand
Her hand, and named her name He could not see. True love can ne'-er for-get

D. C.

Morn to him was dark as night, Yet his heart was full of light, As he this lay be-gan;
Doth a love-ly la-dy land, While the minstrel's love-taught hand, Did o'er his wild harp run;
Fond-ly as when they met, He loved his la-dy yet, His dar-ling one!

INVISIBLE.—All the sounds we hear—the warning noises which keep us from harm, the beautiful musical notes with all the tunes and harmonies that delight us, even the power of hearing the voices of those we love, and learning from one another that which each can tell—all these depend upon the invisible waves of air, even as the pleasures of light depend on the waves of ether. It is by these sound-waves that nature speaks to us, and in all her movements there is a reason why her voice is sharp or tender, loud or gentle, awful or loving. Why does the little brook sing so sweetly, while the wide, deep river makes no noise? Because the little brook eddies and purls round the stones, hitting them as it passes; sometimes the water falls down a large stone, and strikes against the water below, or sometimes it grates the little pebbles together as they lie in its bed. Each of these blows makes a small globe of sound-waves, which spread and spread till they fall on your ear, and because they fall quickly and regularly, they make a low musical note. We might indeed fancy the brook recalling Shelley's beautiful lines:

Sometimes it fell
Among the moss with hollow harmony,
Dark and profound; now on the polished stones
It danced; like childhood laughing as it went.

COME, SING ME THAT SWEET AIR AGAIN.

THOMAS MOORE.

1. Come, sing me that sim - ple air a - gain, I used so to love in life's young
2. Sweet air! how ev - 'ry note brings back Some sun - ny hope, some day - dream

day, And bring, if thou canst, the dreams that then Were wak-en'd by that sweet
bright, That shin - ing o'er life's ear - ly track, Fill'd ev - en its tears with

lay. The ten - der gloom its strain Shed o'er the heart and brow,
light. The new found life that came With love's first ech - o'd vow;

Grief's shadow, with-out its pain, Say . . . where, where is it now? But
The fear, the bliss, the shame, Say . . . where, where are they now? But

play me the well - known air once more, For thoughts of youth still haunt its
still the same lov'd notes pro - long, For sweet 'twere thus to that old

strain, Like dreams of some far fai - ry shore, We're nev - er to see a - gain.
lay, In dreams of youth, and love, and song, To breathe life's hour a - way.

How They Move.—If we are now able to picture to ourselves one set of waves going to the wall, and another set returning and crossing them, we will be ready to understand something of the very difficult question, How is it that we can hear many different sounds at one time and tell them apart? Have you ever watched the sea when its surface is much ruffled, and noticed how, besides the big waves of the tide, there are numberless smaller ripples made by the wind blowing the surface of the water, or the oars of a boat dipping in it, or even rain-drops falling? If you have done this you will have seen that all these waves and ripples cross each other, and you can follow any one ripple with your eye as it goes on its way undisturbed by the rest. Or you may make beautiful crossing and recrossing ripples on a pond by throwing in two stones at a little distance from each other, and here too you can follow any one wave on to the edge of the pond. Now, just in this way the waves of sound, in their manner of moving, cross

OLD ROSIN THE BOW.

Old English Song.

1. I've trav-el'd the wide world o-ver, And now to an-oth-er I'll go; I know that good quar-ters are wait-ing To wel-come old Ros-in the Bow; To wel-come old Ros-in the Bow, . . To welcome old Ros-in the Bow; I know that good quar-ters are wait-ing To wel-come old Ros-in the Bow.

2. And when I am dead, if you wish it, Old friends, you will want to, I know, Come stand by the side of my cof-fin, And look at old Ros-in the Bow; And look at old Ros-in the Bow, . . And look at old Ros-in the Bow; Come stand by the side of my cof-fin, And look at old Ros-in the Bow.

3. Then get you a couple of tombstones, That all who pass by, as they go, May read in the let-ters you put there, The name of old Ros-in the Bow; The name of old Ros-in the Bow, . . The name of old Ros-in the Bow; May read in the let-ters you put there, The name of old Ros-in the Bow.

4. I feel the grim tyrant ap-proaching, That cru-el, im-pla-ca-ble foe, Who spares neither age nor con-di-tion, Nor ev-en old Ros-in the Bow; Nor ev-en old Ros-in the Bow, . . Nor ev-en old Ros-in the Bow; Who spares neither age nor con-di-tion, Not e-ven old Ros-in the Bow.

and recross each other. You will remember too, that different sounds make waves of different lengths, just as the tide makes a long wave and the rain-drops tiny ones. Therefore each sound falls with its own peculiar wave upon your ear, and you can listen to that particular wave just as you look at one particular ripple, and then the sound becomes clear to you.

Audubon, as he camped in the forest, found the song of the whippoorwill one of the most delightful sounds of nature, sweeter to him than that of the nightingale. Musicians have frequently attempted to write out the songs of birds. Wilson Flagg has thus embalmed the songs of nearly all our feathered minstrels. Handel has done kindred work for the nightingale. In the second quartet of the Minuet, Mozart incorporated the cackle of the domestic fowl, while Haydn, in his twentieth quartet, gives, with effect, the joyous note that announces a new-laid egg.

NANCY LEE.

Stephen Adams. C. Matz Arr.

Spirited.

1. Of all the wives as e'er you know, ... Yeo-ho! lads, ho! Yeo-ho! yeo-ho! There's
2. The har-bor's past, the breezes blow, ... Yeo-ho! lads, ho! Yeo-ho! yeo-ho! 'Tis
3. The boa's-'n pipes the watch below, ... Yeo-ho! lads, ho! Yeo-ho! yeo-ho! Then

none like Nancy Lee, I trow, ... Yeo-ho! lads, ho! yeo-ho! ... See
long ere we come back I know, ... Yeo-ho! lads, ho! yeo-ho! ... But
here's a health before we go, ... Yeo-ho! lads, ho! yeo-ho! ... A

there she stands and waves her hands, upon the quay, An' ev'-ry day when I'm away, She'll watch for
true and bright, from morn till night, my home will be, An' all so neat, an' snug, an' sweet, For Jack at
long, long life to my sweet wife, and mates at sea; An' keep our bones from Davy Jones where'er you

me, . An' whisper low, when tempests blow, for Jack at sea, Yeo-ho! lads, ho! . yeo-ho!
sea, . An' Nancy's face to bless the place, an' welcome me; Yeo-ho! lads, ho! . yeo-ho!
be, . An' may you meet a mate as sweet as Nancy Lee. Yeo-ho! lads, ho! . yeo-ho!

The sail-or's wife the sailor's star shall be, Yeo-ho! we go a-cross the

sea, The sail-or's wife the sailor's star shall be, The sailor's wife his star shall be.

II—D

THERE can be no doubt that music has a great influence in imparting those delightful sensations which tend to sweeten and prolong life. That this fact is often recognized is testified by the immense number of those who devote themselves entirely to the manufacture and sale of musical instruments. It is, however, acknowledged throughout the world, that the human voice has no equal for the production of sweet, elevating, enchanting sounds that delight the ear and give tone and coloring to the words of the poet. Hence, of all kinds of music, vocal music should claim the especial attention of all earnest and progressive educators, for singing is known to improve the enunciation, refine the taste, elevate the morals, confirm the health, strengthen the social feeling, and add much to the pleasure of all. The consideration of health is one to which too much attention cannot be given. Singing is beneficial, indirectly, by increasing the flow of spirits, and dispelling weariness and despondency; and directly by the exercise which it gives to the lungs and the vital organs. We cannot sing without increased action of the lungs, and this causes the heart and all the organs of digestion and nutrition, to act with renewed vigor. The singer brings a greater quantity of air into contact with the blood, and hence the blood is better purified and vitalized. Healthful and highly oxygenized blood gives energy to the brain, and thus the mind as well as the body shares the benefit of the exercise. There

THE BROKEN RING.

[DAS ZERBROCHENE RINGLEIN.]

F. GLUCK, 1814.
JOS. VON EICHENDORFF.

1. Far in a shad-ed val-ley A wa-ter-mill ap-pears; But she I love has van-ished From scenes of hap-pier years; But she I love has van-ished From scenes of hap-pier years.
2. She promised to be faith-ful, She pledged it with a ring; But faith-less hath she prov-en, Her gift in twain did spring; But faith-less hath she prov-en, Her gift in twain did spring.
3. How sad-ly now as min-strel Throughout the world I'd roam, My wea-ry bal-lad sing-ing, A-far from friends and home; My wea-ry bal-lad sing-ing, A-far from friends and home.

*4. As soldier would I hasten
Where rages fierce the fight;
And by the watch-fire linger
Through all the gloomy night.

5. Yet whilst the mill I'm hearing
I know not what my mind;
Ah! would my days were ended,
I then should quiet find!

* 4th verse rather fast and *forte*, 5th slower and *pp*.

is great enjoyment in listening to music. As Marx well expresses it: "That which I hear enters into my existence from without, awakens and enriches my mind; but that which I sing is the effluence of my own life, the exertion of my own power to refresh and elevate myself as well as others." Hence all should learn to sing, and children should be taught from their earliest years to sing properly and sweetly. There are parents who imagine that their children have not the power of song. To these I say, in the emphatic words of a teacher of thousands of children and adults, "Most adults and *all* children can learn to sing." The very same organs that are used in speech are used in song, and in almost precisely the same manner. Hence it is obvious that all children who can be taught to talk can likewise be taught to sing. The extent of the ability attained, as a natural consequence, is dependent upon the application of the pupil and the methods of teaching used. And yet singing is almost pre-eminent in its universality, because it is independent of culture. The most ignorant bow to its all-embracing sway, and thousands to whom form and color, science and literature, speak a strange tongue, wake to the familiar accents of the universal language. Their love of it wants no nurture. We cannot prevent their singing, do what we will; and they are likely to feed their lower nature with music if we, as teachers and educators, do not aid them wisely to feed their higher.

WON'T YOU TELL ME WHY, ROBIN?

CLARIBEL.

1. You are not what you were, Rob - in, Why so sad and strange? You
2. On Sun - day, af - ter church, Rob - in, I look'd a - round for you, I
3. The oth - er night we danced, Rob - in, Be - neath the haw - thorn tree; I

once were blithe and gay, Rob - in, What has made you change? You
thought you'd see me home, Rob - in, As once you used to do. But
thought you'd sure - ly come, Rob - in, If but to dance with me; But

nev - er come to see me now, As once you used to do; I miss you at the
now you seem a - fraid to come, And al - most ev - 'ry day I meet you in the
Al - lan asked me first, and so I joined the reel with him; But I was heav - y

wick - et gate, You al - ways let me through, It's ve - ry hard to o - pen, But you
mea - dows, And you look the oth - er way. You nev - er bring me po - sies now, The
heart - ed, And my eyes with tears were dim, And oh, how ve - ry grave you look'd, As

nev - er come to try. ⎫
last is dead and dry. ⎬ Won't you tell me why, Rob - in, Won't you tell me
once we passed you by! ⎭

why? Won't you tell me why, Rob - in, Oh, won't you tell me why?

SILVER CHIMES.

CLARIBEL.

They are chiming gai - ly now, as they chimed so long a - go, Sil - ver tones that we loved so

well;   And what is it that they say To our in - ner thoughts to - day? And

what is the tale that they tell?

1. They whisper first of all, In that qui - et e - ven
2. Of a waking up to life, Of a long and bit - ter
3. Of a peaceful life at last, Of a sense of per - il

fall, Of the hap - py days of childhood that we passed;   When each
strife, Of a rest - less spir - it fret - ting in its pain;   Of a
past, Of a fu - ture left in saf - er hands than ours;   Of a

gar - land that we made, Seem'd too beau - ti - ful to fade; And each but - ter - fly more
sea - son when the bells On - ly racked us with their spells, On - ly mocked us with old
sweet, re - fresh - ing dew, Fall - ing on our lives a - new, As the rain - drops fall and

D.S. After last stanza.

ra - diant than the last, the last.
mem - o - ries a - gain, a - gain.
sat - is - fy the flowers, the flowers.

They are chiming gai - ly now, As they

chimed so long a - go, Sil - ver tones that we loved so well. Like a

rit. *dim.* *pp*

sto - ry that is told, Seem those memories of old, Haunting still with a mag-ic spell, magic spell.

MY NORMANDY.

FREDERIC BERAT.

Andante.

1. When hope her cheering smile supplies, And win-ter flies far, far a-way; Be-
2. I've seen Hel-ve - tia's flow-ery fields, Its cot-tag-es, its i - cy hills; And
3. There is an age in all our lives, When ev-ry dream must lose its spell; An

neath, dear France, thy beauteous skies, When spring becomes more sweet and gay; When
I - ta - ly, thy sky so clear! And Ven-ice, with her gon - do-lier. In
age in which the soul re - calls The scenes o'er which it loved to dwell; When

na-ture's dressed a - gain in green, The swal-low to re - turn is seen; I
greet-ing thus each for-eign part, There's still one land most near my heart, A
e'en my muse shall si - lent prove, Per-haps de-spise these songs of love,— 'Tis

love a - gain the land to see, Which gave me, gave me birth, my Nor-man-dy.
land most cherished, loved by me, My na-tive, na-tive land, my Nor-man-dy.
then I hope the land to see, Which gave me, gave me birth, my Nor-man-dy.

THE MOONLIGHT SONATA.—The *Wide-Awake Magazine* tells a pretty story of the way that Beethoven composed this beautiful piece of music. He was going by a small house one evening and heard some one playing his Symphony in F on the Piano. He stopped to listen, and heard a voice say: "What would I not give to hear that piece played by some one who could do it justice." The great composer opened the door and entered. "Pardon me," said Beethoven, somewhat embarrassed; "pardon me, but I heard music, and was tempted to enter. I am a musician!" The girl blushed, and the young man assumed a grave, almost severe manner. "I heard also some of your words," continued Beethoven. "You wish to hear, that is, you would like—in short,

would you like me to play to you?" There was something so strange, so comical in the whole affair, and something so agreeable and eccentric in Beethoven's manner, that we all involuntarily smiled. "Thank you," said the young shoemaker; "but our piano is bad, and then we have no music." "No music?" repeated Beethoven, "how, then, did mademoiselle—." He stopped and colored, for the young girl had just turned towards him, and by her sad, veiled eyes he saw that she was blind. "I entreat you to pardon me," stammered he; "but I did not remark at first. You play, then, from memory?" "Entirely!" "And where have you heard this music before?" "Never, excepting the music in the streets." She seemed frightened, so Beethoven did not

NONE CAN TELL.

W. H. EMRA. G. B. ALLEN.

1. Child, is life bright a - lone? None can tell. Al - ways laugh - ter, nev - er moan? None can tell. Will spring flow'rets bloom as sweet, Un - der care - less rov - ing feet, Or lie with-er'd with the heat? None can tell, None can tell.

2. Youth, is she tru - ly thine? None can tell. Will love's light e - ter - nal shine? None can tell. Will the sun make glad thy day, Or will black clouds hide his ray, And love's ten - der beams de - cay? None can tell, None can tell.

3. Bride, is there joy for thee? None can tell. Or will blue skies cloud - ed be? None can tell. Will the bright dream ne'er depart, Or will grief, with last - ing smart, Keep a dull grasp on thy heart? None can tell, None can tell.

add another word, but seated himself at the instrument and began to play. He had not touched many notes when I guessed, says the narrator, who accompanied him, what would follow, and how sublime he would be that evening. I was not deceived. Never, during the many years I knew him, did I hear him play as on this occasion for the blind girl and her brother on that old dilapidated piano. At last the shoemaker rose, approached him, and said in a low voice: "Wonderful man, who are you then?" Beethoven raised his head, as if he had not comprehended. The young man repeated the question. The composer smiled as only he could smile. "Listen," said he; and he played the first movement in the F Symphony. A cry of joy escaped

from the lips of the brother and sister. They recognized the player and cried: "You are, then, Beethoven!" He rose to go, but they detained him. "Play for us once more, just once more." He allowed himself to be led back to the instrument. The brilliant rays of the moon entered the curtainless windows and lighted up his broad, earnest, and expressive forehead. "I am going to improvise a sonata to the moonlight," he said, playfully. He contemplated for some moments the sky sparkling with stars; then his fingers rested on the piano, and he began to play in a low, sad, but wondrously sweet strain. The harmony issued from the instrument as sweet and even as the bright rays of the beautiful moonlight spread over the shadows on the ground.

EVER OF THEE.

G. LINLEY.
FOLEY HALL.

Moderato.

1. Ev - er of thee I'm fond - ly dream - ing. Thy gen - tle voice my
2. Ev - er of thee, when sad and lone - ly, Wand-'ring a - far my

spir - it can cheer; Thou art the star that, mild - ly beam - ing, Shone o'er my path when
soul joy'd to dwell; Ah! then I felt I loved thee on - ly, All seemed to fade be-

all was dark and drear: Still in my heart thy form I cher - ish,
fore af - fec - tion's spell; Years have not chill'd the love I cher - ish,

Ev -'ry kind tho't like a bird flies to thee. Ah! nev - er till life and mem-'ry per - ish,
True as the stars hath my heart been to thee. Ah! nev - er till life and mem-'ry per - ish,

Can I for - get how dear thou art to me: Morn, noon and night, where'er I may be,
Can I for - get how dear thou art to me: Morn, noon and night, where'er I may be,

ad lib.

Fond - ly I'm dream-ing ev - er of thee; Fond - ly I'm dream-ing ev - er of thee.
Fond - ly I'm dream-ing ev - er of thee; Fond - ly I'm dream-ing ev - er of thee.

ECHOES.—Try to imagine that you see the sound-waves spreading all around you, striking on your ears as they pass, then on the ears of those behind you, and on and on in widening globes till they reach the wall. What will happen when they get there? If the wall were thin, as a wooden partition is, they would shake it, and it again would shake the air on the other side, and so any one in the next room would have the sound of my voice brought to their ear. But something more will happen. In any case the sound-waves hitting against the wall will bound back from it just as a ball bounds back when thrown against any hard surface, and so another set of sound-waves reflected from the wall will come back across the room. If these waves come to your ear so quickly that they mix with direct waves, they help to make the sound louder. For instance, if I say " Ha," you hear that sound louder in this room than you would in the open air, for the " Ha" from my mouth and a second " Ha" from the wall come to your ear so instantaneously that they make one sound. This is why you can often hear better at the far end of the church when you stand against a screen or a wall, than when you are halfway up the building nearer the speaker, because near the wall the reflected waves strike strongly on your ear and thus make the sound louder. Sometimes, when the sound comes from a great explosion, as of gunpowder or dynamite, these reflected waves are so strong that they are able to break glass. Now, suppose the

HE GIVETH HIS BELOVED SLEEP.

FRANZ ABT.
T. C. TILDESLEY.

1. Sor-row and care may meet,   The tem-pest cloud may low'r,   The surge of sin may
   din   of war may roll,   With all her rag-ing flight,   Grief may oppress the
   child-hood's winsome page,   In man-hood's joy-ous bloom,   In feeble-ness and

beat   Up-on earth's trou-bled shore;   God doth His own in safe-ty keep,
soul,   Throughout the wea-ry night;   God doth His own in safe-ty keep,
age,   In death's dark gathering gloom,   God will His own in safe-ty keep,

He giv-eth His be-lov-ed sleep, He giv-eth His be-lov- - -ed sleep. 2. The
He giv-eth His be-lov-ed sleep, He giv-eth His be-lov- - -ed sleep. 3. In
He giv-eth His be-lov-ed sleep, He giv-eth His be-lov- - -ed sleep.

wall were so far behind you that the reflected sound-waves hit upon your ear only after those coming straight from me had died away; then you would hear the sound twice, " Ha" from me and " Ha" from the wall, and here you have an echo, " Ha, ha." For this to happen in ordinary air, you must be standing at least 56 feet away from the point from which the waves are reflected, as then the second blow will come one-tenth of a second after the first, and that is long enough for you to feel them separately. Miss Martineau tells a story of a dog that was terribly frightened by an echo. Thinking another dog was barking, he ran forward to meet him, and was very much astonished when, as he came nearer the wall, the echo ceased. I myself once knew a case of this kind, and my dog, when he could find no enemy, ran back barking, till he was a certain distance off, and then the echo, of course, began again. He grew so furious at last that we had much difficulty in preventing him from flying at a strange man who happened to be passing at the time. Sometimes, in the mountains, walls of rock rise at some distance one behind another, and their each one will send back its echo a little later than the rock before it, so that the " Ha" which you give will come back as a peal of laughter. There is an echo in Woodstock Park which repeats the word twenty times. Again sometimes, as in the Alps, the sound-waves in coming back rebound from mountain to mountain and are driven backwards and forwards, becoming fainter and fainter till they die away. These echoes are very beautiful.—*Buckley.*

CROWN HIM WITH MANY CROWNS.

M. Bridges.
G. J. Elvey. "Diademata."

1. Crown Him with ma - ny crowns, The Lamb up - on His throne; Hark! how the heavenly
2. Crown Him the Lord of Love! Be-hold His hands and side,—Those wounds, yet vis - i -
3. Crown Him the Lord of Peace! Whose power a scep - tre sways In heaven and earth, that
4. Crown Him the Lord of Heaven! One with the Fa - ther known,—And the blest Spir - it,

an - them drowns All mu - sic but its own! A - wake, my soul, and sing Of
ble a - bove, In beau - ty glo - ri - fied: No an - gel in the sky Can
wars may cease, And all be prayer and praise. His reign shall know no end; And
through Him given From yon-der Tri - une throne! All hail, Re - deem - er, hail! For

Him who died for thee; And hail Him as thy matchless King Through all eter - ni - ty.
ful - ly bear that sight, But downward bends his wondering eye At myster-ies so bright.
round His pier-cèd feet, Fair flowers of Par - a - dise ex - tend Their fragrance ev-er sweet.
Thou hast died for me: Thy praise and glo-ry shall not fail Throughout e - ter - ni - ty.

THE CHAPEL.

Words by Uhland.

1. See yon chap - el on the hill, Calm it looks o'er all the plain;
2. Sad - ly chants the choir a - long; Sad - ly sounds the chap - el bell;
3. Those who once had smiled in joy, To the bur - ial there they bring;

Cheer - ful - ly by mead and rill, Sings the shep - herd boy his strain.
Hush'd is now the shep - herd's song, And he lis - tens in the dell.
Shep - herd boy! Oh, shep - herd boy! O'er thee too they yet will sing.

INFLUENCE OF MUSIC.—Man is as much a child of the beautiful as he is of wisdom or genius, Nature never drives us if she can avoid it; she prefers to allure us. She makes all things charming. She paints the fields and the woods that we may go to them, led by affection. She makes the face of youth beautiful, throws color on the cheek, and makes the lines of smiles and laughter come and go, and she sends the soul into the eyes, that young years may build up everlasting frienship. Yielding to his Divine Master's guidance, man follows the beautiful, and to the idea of home or temple or garden or city, he comes with both hands full of ornament. He claims for his house and his dress what God gives to the peach, or the leaf, or the rose. In this deep philosophy music comes as the decoration of a thought. Man submits his truths to several steps of this ennobling work. He found them in prose and he asks Milton or Dante, or Tennyson or Longfellow to frame them into poetry, but not yet satisfied

I'VE BEEN ROAMING.

CHAS. E. HORN.

Lively.

1. I've been roam-ing, I've been roam-ing Where the mea-dow dew is sweet;
2. I've been roam-ing, I've been roam-ing By the rose and lil-y fair;
3. I've been roam-ing, I've been roam-ing Where the hon-ey-suc-kle creeps;
4. I've been roam-ing, I've been roam-ing O-ver hill and o-ver plain;

And I'm com-ing, and I'm com-ing With its pearls up-on my feet,
And I'm com-ing, and I'm com-ing With their blos-soms in my hair, I've been
And I'm com-ing, and I'm com-ing With its greet-ing on my lips,
And I'm com-ing, and I'm com-ing To my bow-er back a-gain, O-ver

roam-ing, I've been roam-ing Where the mea-dow dew is sweet,
(4) hill, and o-ver plain, To my bow-er back a-gain,

And I'm com-ing, and I'm com-ing With its pearls up-on my feet.
(4) And I'm com-ing, and I'm com-ing To my bow-er back a-gain.

he takes the thought to the great musician and asks Mozart or Weber or Schubert to pour still more color on the blessed thought. It was not enough for the Greeks that some of their truth took the poetic form of the drama, it must also be sung on the stage, so that between the uplifted hands of both Poetry and Music all might see how sorrowful was Œdipus or how sweet Antigone. Thus all through its history, music has ever been the final decoration of a sentiment. Poetry has done much when it has gathered up some of the pensive meditations of man when he draws near his long home and has called this rhythmical arrangement a poem. Even read to us, its flow of harmonious feet is impressive; but when Mozart goes further, and wreathes those words with his composition into a requiem, then is the cup of our realization full, and all the pomp and splendor of earth sink like the summer sun.—*Swing.*

FLOW GENTLY, SWEET AFTON.

J. E. SPILMAN.
Words by ROBERT BURNS.

1. Flow gent-ly, sweet Af-ton, a-mang thy green braes; Flow gent-ly, I'll sing thee a
2. How loft-ly, sweet Af-ton, thy neighbor-ing hills, Far marked with the courses of
3. Thy crys-tal stream, Af-ton, how love-ly it glides, And winds by the cot where my

song in thy praise; My Ma-ry's a-sleep by thy murmur-ing stream, Flow gent-ly, sweet
clear-winding rills; There dai-ly I wan-der, as morn ris-es high, My flocks and my
Ma-ry re-sides! How wan-ton thy wa-ters her snow-y feet lave, As gath'ring sweet

Af-ton, dis-turb not her dream. Thou stock-dove, whose e-cho re-sounds from the
Ma-ry's sweet cot in my eye, How pleas-ant thy banks and green val-leys be-
flowerets, she stems thy clear wave! Flow gent-ly, sweet Af-ton, a-mang thy green

hill, Ye wild whistling black-birds in yon thorn-y den, Thou green-crest-ed
low, Where wild in the woodlands the prim-ros-es blow! There oft, as mild
braes, Flow gent-ly, sweet riv-er, the theme of my lays: My Ma-ry's a-

lap-wing, thy screaming for-bear, I charge you, dis-turb not my slum-ber-ing fair.
evening creeps o-ver the lea, The sweet-scented birk shades my Ma-ry and me.
sleep by thy mur-mur-ing stream, Flow gent-ly, sweet Af-ton, dis-turb not her dream.

HYMN TUNES.—The tunes which burden our modern books, in hundreds and thousands, utterly devoid of character, without meaning or substance, may be sung a hundred times, and not a person in the congregation will remember them.   There is nothing to remember.   They are the very emptiness of fluent noise.   But let a true tune be sung, and every person of sensibility, every person of feeling, every child even, is aroused and touched.   The melody clings to them.   On the way home snatches of it will be heard on this side and on that; and when the next Sabbath, the same song is heard, one and another of the people fall in, and the volume grows with each verse, until at length the song, breaking forth as a many-rilled stream from the hills, grows deeper and flows on, broad as a mighty river! Such tunes are never forgotten.   They cling to us through our whole life.   We carry them with us upon our journey. We sing them in the forest.   The workman follows the plow with sacred songs. Children catch them, and singing only for the joy it gives them now, are yet laying up for all their life food of the

JESUS, LOVER OF MY SOUL.

FRANZ. ART.
CHAS. WESLEY, 1740.

1. Je - sus, lov - er of my soul, Let me to Thy bo - som fly, While the
2. Oth - er ref - uge have I none; Hangs my help - less soul on Thee; Leave, ah!
3. Plen-teous grace with Thee is found, Grace to par - don all my sin; Let the

bil - lows near me roll, While the tem-pest still is high! Hide me, O my Sa - viour, hide,
leave me not a - lone, Still sup - port and com-fort me! All my trust on Thee is stayed,
heal-ing streams abound; Make and keep me pure with-in! Thou of life the Fountain art,

Till the storms of life are past; Safe in to the ha - ven guide;
All my help from Thee I bring; Cov - er - my de - fence - less head
Free-ly let me take of Thee; Spring Thou up with - in my heart!

Oh, re - ceive my soul at last! Oh, re - ceive my soul at last!
With the shad - ow of Thy wing! With the shad - ow of Thy wing!
Rise to all e - ter - ni - ty! Rise to all e - ter - ni - ty.

sweetest joy.   Such tunes give new harmony and sweetness even to the hymns which float upon their current.   And when some celestial hymn of Wesley or of the scarcely less than inspired Watts, is wafted upon such music, the soul is lifted up above all its ailments and rises into the very presence of God, with joys no longer unspeakable, though full of glory. In selecting music, we should not allow any fastidiousness of taste to set aside the lessons of experience. A tune which has always interested a congregation, which inspires the young, and lends to enthusiasm a fit expression, ought not to be set aside because it does not follow the reigning fashion or conform to the whims of technical science.   There is such a thing as Pharisaism in music. Tunes may be faulty in structure, and yet convey a full-hearted current that will sweep out of the way the worthless, heartless trash whose only merit is a literal correctness.   When a tune has been found to do good work, it should be used for what it does and can do.—*H. W. Beecher.*

QUIET, LORD, MY FROWARD HEART.

W. H. Monk.
John Newton, 1779.

1. Qui - et, Lord, my fro - ward heart, Make me teach - a - ble and mild,
2. What Thou shalt to - day pro - vide, Let me as a child re - ceive;
3. As a lit - tle child re - lies On a care be - yond his own,

Up - right, sim - ple, free from art, Make me as a lit - tle child;
What to - mor - row may be - tide, Calm - ly to Thy wis - dom leave;
Knows he's neith - er strong nor wise, Fears to stir or step a - lone,

From dis - trust and en - vy free, Pleased with all that pleas - es Thee.
'Tis e - nough that Thou wilt care; Why should I the bur - den bear?
Let me thus with Thee a - bide As my Fath - er, Guard, and Guide.

GENTLY LEAD US.

Thos. Hastings.
Ithamar Conkey. "Rathbun.
By per. O. Ditson & Co.

1. Gent - ly, Lord, oh gent - ly lead us Through this gloom - y vale of tears:
2. When temp - ta - tion's darts as - sail us When in de - vious paths we stray,
3. In the hour of pain and an - guish, In the hour when death draws near,
4. When this mor - tal life is end - ed, Bid us in Thine arms to rest,

Thro' the chang - es Thou'st de - creed us, Till our last great change ap - pears.
Let Thy good - ness nev - er fail us, Lead us in thy per - fect way.
Suf - fer not our hearts to lan - guish, Suf - fer not our souls to fear.
Till by an - gel bands at - tend - ed, We a - wake a - mong the blest.

THE MAY QUEEN.

ALFRED TENNYSON.
WM. R. DEMPSTER, 1845.

1. You must wake and call me ear - ly, call me ear - ly, moth - er dear; To -
2. Lit - tle Ef - fie shall go with me to-mor - row to the green, And
3. The night winds come and go, moth - er, up-on the mead-ow grass, And

mor - row will be the hap-pi - est time of all the glad New Year; Of
you'll be there too, moth - - er, to see me made the Queen; There
the hap-py stars a - bove them seem to bright-en as they pass; There

all the glad New Year, moth - er, the mad - dest, mer - ri - est day: For
shep - herd lads on ev - 'ry side will come from far a - way, For
will not be a drop o' rain the whole o' the live - long day, For

I'm to be Queen o' the May, mother, I'm to be Queen o' the May. I
I'm to be Queen o' the May, mother, I'm to be Queen o' the May. All
I'm to be Queen o' the May, mother, I'm to be Queen o' the May. So you must

sleep so sound all night, moth - er, that I shall nev - er a - wake, If you
the val - ley, moth - er, will be fresh and green and still, And the
wake and call me ear - ly, call me ear - ly, moth - er dear, To -

do not call me loud when the day be - gins to break: But
cow - slip and the crow - foot are o - ver all the hill, The
mor - row'll be the happiest time of all the glad New Year, To -

By permission Oliver Ditson & Company, Boston.

I must gath-er knots of flowers, and buds and gar - lands gay, For
rivulet in the flow - 'ry dale will mer - ri - ly glance and play For
morrow'll be of all the year, the mad - dest mer-ri-est yet, For

I'm to be Queen o' the May, moth-er, I'm to be Queen o' the May.

"GOOD-BYE."

J. C. ENGELBRECHT.

1. Farewell, fare-well is a lone - ly sound And al - ways brings a sigh, But
2. Farewell, fare-well may do for the gay, When pleas-ure's throng is nigh, But

give to me when loved ones part, That sweet old word, "good - bye," That
give to me that bet - ter word, That comes from the heart, "good - bye," That

sweet old word, "good - bye," That sweet old word "good - bye," But
comes from the heart, "good-bye," That comes from the heart, "good-bye," But

give to me, when loved ones part, That sweet old word, "good - bye."
give to me that bet - ter word, That comes from the heart, "good-bye."

Adieu, adieu we hear it oft
  With a tear, perhaps with a sigh,
But the heart feels most when the lips move not,
  And the eye speaks the gentle "good-bye,"

Farewell, farewell, is never heard,
  When the tear's in the mother's eye,
Adieu, adieu, she speaks it not,
  But, "My love, good-bye, good-bye,"

HYMN WRITERS.—We have sought for hymns in the books of every denomination of Christians. There are certain hymns of the sacrifice of Christ, of utter and almost soul-dissolving yearning for the benefits of His mediation, which none could write so well as a devout Roman Catholic. Some of the most touching and truly evangelical hymns in the Plymouth Collection we have gathered from this source. We have obtained many exquisite hymns from the Moravian collections, developing the most tender and loving views of Christ, of His personal presence, and gentle companionship. We know of no hymn-writers that equal their faith and fervor for Christ as present with his people. Nor can any one conversant with these fail to recognize the fountain in which the incomparable Charles Wesley was baptized. His hymns are only Moravian hymns re-sung. Not alone are the favorite expressions used and the epithets which they loved, but, like them, he beholds all Christian truths through the medium of confiding love. The *love-element* of this school has never been surpassed. To say that we have sought for hymns expressing the deepest religious feeling, and particularly the sentiments of love, and trust, and divine courage, and

FLEE AS A BIRD.

SPANISH MELODY.
MARY S. B. DANA, 1840.

Expression.

1. Flee as a bird to your moun - tain, Thou who art wea - ry of sin; . . . Go to the clear-flowing foun - tain, Where you may wash and be clean; Fly, for th' a-venger is near thee, Call, and the Sav - iour will hear thee, He on His bo - som will bear thee; Oh, thou who art wea - ry of sin, Oh, thou who art wea - ry of sin.

2. He will protect thee for - ev - er, Wipe ev - e - ry fall - ing tear; . . . He will forsake thee, Oh, nev - er, Sheltered so ten-der - ly there! Haste then, the hours are fly - ing, Spend not the mo - ments in sigh - ing, Cease from your sor - row and cry - ing, The Sav-iour will wipe ev - 'ry tear, The Sav-iour will wipe ev - 'ry tear,

hopefulness, is only to say that we have drawn largely from the best Methodist hymns. The contributions of the Wesleys to hymnology have been so rich as to leave the Christian world under an obligation which cannot be paid as long as there is a struggling Christian brotherhood to sing and be comforted amid the trials of this world. Charles Wesley was peculiarly happy in making the Scriptures illustrate Christian experience, and personal experience throw light upon the deep places of the Bible. Some of his effusions have never been surpassed. Nor are there any hymns that could more nobly express the whole ecstasy of the apostolic writings in view of death and heaven. Cowper, Stennet, Newton, Doddridge, and many other familiar authors, will be found in every collection that aspires to usefulness. With whatever partiality to Dr. Watts we may have begun our work, a comparison of his psalms and hymns with the best effusions of the best hymn-writers has only served to increase our admiration, and our conviction that he stands above all other English writers. Nor do we believe any other man, in any department, has contributed so great a share of enjoyment, edification, and inspiration to struggling Christians as Dr. Watts.—*H. W. Beecher.*

PRAISE TO GOD.

ANNA L. BARBAULD, 1773.
SEBASTIAN BACH. "NUREMBERG."

1. Praise to God, im-mor-tal praise, For the love that crowns our days;
2. Flocks that whit-en all the plain, Yel-low sheaves of ri-pened grain,
3. All that spring, with boun-teous hand, Scat-ters o'er the smil-ing land;
4. Lord, for these our souls shall raise Grate-ful vows and sol-emn praise:

Boun-teous source of ev-'ry joy! Let Thy praise our tongues em-ploy.
Clouds that drop their fattening dews, Suns that tem-perate warmth dif-fuse.
All that lib-eral au-tumn pours From her rich, o'er-flow-ing stores:
And, when ev-'ry bles-sing's flown, Love Thee for Thy-self a-lone.

RISE, CROWNED WITH LIGHT.

ALEXANDER POPE.
ALEXIS LVOFF. "RUSSIAN HYMN."

1. Rise, crown'd with light, . . im-pe-rial Sa-lem, rise; Ex-alt thy
2. See a long race . . thy spa-cious courts a-dorn, See fu-ture
3. See barbarous na . . tions at thy gates at-tend, Walk in thy
4. The seas shall waste, . . the skies to smoke de-cay, Rocks fall to

tow'r-ing head and lift thine eyes; See Heav'n its spark-ling por-tals
sons, and daugh-ters yet un-born, In crowding ranks on ev-'ry
light, and in thy tem-ple bend; See thy bright al-tars throng'd with
dust, and mountains melt a-way; But fix'd His word, His sav-ing

wide . . . dis-play, And break up-on thee in a flood of day.
side . . . a-rise, De-mand-ing life, im-pa-tient for the skies.
pros . . . trate kings, While ev-'ry land its joy-ous tri-bute brings.
pow'r . . . re-mains, Thy realm shall last, thy own Mes-si-ah reign.

A HYMN is a lyrical discourse to the feelings. It should either excite or express feeling. The recitation of historical facts, descriptions of scenery, narrations of events, meditations, all may tend to inspire feeling. Hymns are not to be excluded, therefore, because they are deficient in lyrical form, or in feeling, if experience shows that they have power to excite pious emotions. Not many of Newton's hymns can be called poetical; yet there are few hymns in the English language that are more useful. Scarcely any two ministers would agree in the selection of hymns. A collection should be made so large and various that every one may find in it that which he needs. Neither should one complain of the multitude of hymns useless to *him*. They are not useless to others. A generously spread table is not at fault because, in the profusion, each guest cannot use everything. Every one should have all

the liberty and the means of following his own taste. Hymn-books have often been so fastidiously made, as not only to exclude many hymns, as extravagant, that were not half so extravagant as are the Psalms of David, and as is all true and deep feeling which gives itself full expression; but also those retained have been abused by corrections, so called, and tamed down from their noble fervor and careless freedom, into flat and profitless propriety. No language can well replace that which the original inspiration of the author suggested.—*H. W. Beecher.*

ONE evening, I found Felix Mendelssohn deep in the Bible, "Listen," he said, and then he read to me, in a gentle and agitated voice, the passage from the First Book of Kings, beginning with the words, "And behold the Lord passed by." "Would not that be splendid for an oratorio?" he exclaimed; and it did become part of his work, the Elijah.—*Hiller.*

KINDRED HEARTS.

GERMAN.
FELICIA HEMANS.

1. Oh, ask not, hope not thou too much Of sym - pa - thy be - low, Few are the hearts whence once a touch Bids the sweet fountains flow; Few, and by still con - flict-ing powers Forbid-den here to meet; Such ties would make this life of ours Too fair for aught so fleet, Too fair for aught so fleet.

2. The tune that speaks of oth - er times, A sor - row - ful de - light, The mel - o - dy of dis - tant chimes, The sound of waves by night, The wind that with so many a tone Some chord within can thrill,— These may have lan-guage all thine own, To him a mys - ter - y still, To him a mys - ter - y still.

3. Yet scorn thou not, for this, the true And stead - fast love of years, The kind - ly that from childhood grew, The faith - ful to thy tears. If there be one that o'er the dead Hath in thy grief borne part, And watch'd through sickness by thy bed, Call his a kin - dred heart, Call his a kin - dred heart.

4. But for those bonds all per - fect made, Wherein bright spir - its blend, Like sis - ter flow'rs of one sweet shade, With the same breeze that bend, For that full bliss of thought allied Nev - er to mor - tals given,— Oh lay thy love - ly dreams aside, Or lift them in - to heaven, Or lift them in - to heaven.

THE LIGHT IN THE WINDOW.

LONSDALE.
VIRGINIA GABRIEL.

p

1. One long, last kiss at the shiel - ing door, Ere he sad - ly passed down the
2. She fold - ed his homespun suit of grey, And gath - ered sweet wild thyme to
3. Long years had sped, but the light gleam'd still Through the sum - mer star - light and

cres.

moun - tain path, And she saw her sol - dier boy no more Till he
lay be - tween, And hung his crook in the old fond way, She used
win - try frost, Ere Co - lin climbed up the mist - wreath'd hill, And her

pp

march'd with his com - rades up the strath. Their tar - tan plaids and their
when her Col - in came home at e'en. When gloam - ing fell and the
fond arms cir - cled the boy she lost, "Oh wel - come, dar - ling, though

cres.

plumes grew dim, But the wail of the pi - broch e - cho - ed shrill, As
wheel was dumb, She lit her dim lamp at the win-dow pane, Though
late, so late, Let me kiss you, sweet! ere my spir - it flies To

con espressione.   *dim.*   *rit.*   *a tempo.*

soft - ly breath - ing a pray-er for him, She turn'd to her home on the
she knew her lad - die ne'er would come, From herd - ing his sheep on the
watch at the win-dows of heaven, and wait Thy [*Omit.*]

3rd verse.

heath - clad hill.
hills a - gain.   feet at the thres - hold of Pa - ra - dise.

The influence of music upon a pure mind cannot be understood in this life, much less expressed. The teacher who introduces music into the school as a regular exercise, will have better discipline and will himself be better. It quickens thought in the students and relieves the monotony of routine, Teach the student to read by note, if possible. If you have no books, use the fingers for notes. Take a given pitch—as C, as a standard. Tell your pupils that to sing they must put into action a vocal reed organ, with lungs as bellows, the wind-pipe as pipe, vocal chords as reeds, tongue as the bridge, the roof of the mouth as sounding board. Ask them to define a tone, allowing them to express their own ideas. Illustrate by means of a piece of rubber stretched and vibrated; thus teach them that sound is vibration collected and reflected from anything that produces sound. Illustrate lines, spaces, rests, and so on through the fundamental principles. Inform yourselves thoroughly here. Be not like soldiers on a long march with rations for only a few days. Be true to your calling. It is said that Michael Angelo, while at his work, wore fastened to the forepiece of his artist's cap a lighted candle that no shadow of himself might fall upon his work. This custom spoke a more eloquent lesson than he knew, How often the shadows fall upon our work—falling from ourselves!—*Russel.*

THE LONG WEARY DAY.

(DEN LIEBEN LANGEN TAG.)

SUABIAN VOLKSLIED.

1. The long, long wea-ry day, In tears is passed a-way, The long, long weary day, In tears is passed a-way, Yet still at even-ing I am weeping, As from my window's height, I look out on the night; I still am weep-ing, My lone watch keep-ing; As from my window's height, I look out on the night; I still am weep-ing, My lone watch keep-ing.

2. For oh! my love is dead; To Heav'n his soul is sped. For oh! my love is dead; To Heav'n his soul is sped. For him, with heart and soul I'm weeping; To see him nev-er more, It grieves my heart so sore! I still am weep-ing, My lone watch keep-ing, To see him nev-er more, It grieves my heart so sore! I still am weep-ing, My lone watch keep-ing.

3. When I, his truth to prove, Would trifle with his love, When I, his truth to prove, Would trifle with his love, He'd say, "Thou shalt for me be weeping Up-on some fu-ture day, When I am far a-way, Thou shalt be weep-ing, Thy lone watch keep-ing; Up-on some fu-ture day, When I am far a-way, Thou shalt be weep-ing, Thy lone watch keep-ing."

4. Had naught but land or sea
Parted my love from me,
I should not now sad tears be weeping;
But hope he'd come once more,
And love me as of yore,
And say, "Cease weeping,
Thy lone watch keeping,"

5. Now comes he nevermore!
It grieves me, ah! so sore!
And still at evening am I weeping;
When the stars above appear,
I see his eyes so clear;
My lone watch keeping,
I still am weeping.

OH, SACRED HEAD, ONCE WOUNDED.

GREEK MELODY.
BERNARD, A. D. 1153.

1. Oh, sacred, Head once wounded, With grief and shame weigh'd down; Now scornfully sur-
2. What Thou, my Lord, hast suffered Was all for sin-ners' gain; Mine, mine was the trans-
3. What language shall I bor - row To thank Thee, dearest Friend, For 'this Thy dy - ing
4. Be near me when I'm dy - ing, Oh, show Thy cross to me! And for my suc-cor

round - ed With thorns Thine on-ly crown; Oh, sa - cred Head, what glo - ry, What
gres - sion, But Thine the dead - ly pain: Lo, here I fall, my Sav - iour! 'Tis
sor - row, Thy pi - ty with - out end? Oh, make me Thine for - ev - er; And
fly - ing, Come, Lord, and set me free! These eyes, new faith re - ceiv - ing, From

bliss, till now was Thine! Yet though despised and go - ry, I joy to call Thee mine.
I de-serve Thy place; Look on me with Thy fav - or, Vouchsafe to me Thy grace.
should I faint-ing be, Lord, let me nev - er, nev - er, Out - live my love for Thee!
Je - sus shall not move; For he who dies be - liev - ing, Dies safe-ly, through Thy love.

TO THY PASTURES FAIR AND LARGE.

J. MERRICK.

1. To Thy pas - tures fair and large, Heav'n - ly Shep - herd, lead Thy charge,
2. When I faint with sum - mer's heat, Thou shalt guide my wea - ry feet
3. Safe the drear - y vale I tread, By the shades of death o'er - spread,
4. Con - stant to my lat - est end, Thou my foot - steps shalt at - tend;

And my couch, with tend - 'rest care, Mid the spring - ing grass pre-pare.
To the streams that still and slow, Through the ver - dant mead-ows flow.
With Thy rod and staff sup - plied, This my guard, and that my guide.
And shalt bid Thy hal - low'd dome Yield me an e - ter - nal home.

GRADUALLY, in Italy, singing became an art. What we mean by singing when we speak of it as a source of pleasure of the higher kind, is really an Italian art, which has been diffused over the civilized world; and the Italian school of singing is still the great school.—others, in so far as they differ from that school, being inferior. The first distinctive characteristic of the Italian school of singing is the delivery of the voice, the mode of uttering a single note. Italians generally (for singing in this way has become a second nature to the whole people) use their voices in quite a different way from the generality of other people. They naturally utter their notes with a purity and a freedom rarely heard from untaught persons of other races. This delivery of the voice is the foundation of their excellence as singers. Indeed, it may almost be said to constitute that excellence; for not only is there no great singing without it, but the chief end of Italian vocal discipline is to attain execution united with this free vocal utterance.

THE SLUMBER-SONG.

F. KÜCKEN.

Very Slow.

1. { All is still in sweet - est rest, Be thy sleep se - rene - ly blest!
   { *Al - les still in süs - ser Ruh! D'rum mein Kind so schlaf auch du!*

2. { Close each lit - tle, lov - ing eye, Let them like two rose - lets lie;
   { *Schlies-se dei - ne Aeu - ge-lein, Lass sie wie zwei Knos - pen sein!*

Winds are moan - ing o'er the wild, Lul - la - by, sleep on, my child;
Draus-sen säu - selt nur der Wind, Su, su, su! schlaf ein, mein Kind:
And when pur - pling morn shall glow, Still as rose - lets fresh - ly blow,
Mor - gen wenn die Sonn' er - glüht, Sind sie wie die Blum' er - blüht,

Lul - la - by, sleep on, my child, La, lul - la - by, sleep on, my
Su, su, su! schlaf ein, mein Kind; Su, su, su, su! schlaf ein, mein
Still as rose - lets fresh - ly blow; La, lul - la - by, sleep on, my
Sind sie wie die Blum' er - blüht, Su, su, su, su! schlaf ein,

child; May an - gel gleams Per - vade thy dreams! . . . . .
Kind: Su, su, su, su! In gu - ter Ruh'! . . . . . .

There are singers who have voices of remarkable power, range and flexibility, who can never be great because, either by nature or from bad and ineradicable habit, they cannot attain this pure and free delivery of the voice. Their tone is guttural, or it is nasal, or it is rough, or it is unsteady, or something else; it may be merely constrained; in any case, the fault is more or less destructive. There may be great singing without great power, without remarkable flexibility, without the ability to execute a roulade or trill; but there can be no singing really great without this free, pure delivery of the voice. A singer who can go through the whole range of his voice, from low to high, swelling out the tone and diminishing it with the vowel sound of broad *a* (ah,) preserving that sound pure, and uniting with it perfect intonation through crescendo and diminuendo, has conquered much more than half the difficulties of the art of vocalization. All the rest, almost without exception, are mere "limbs and outward flourishes."

SHALL WE MEET BEYOND THE RIVER?

H. L. Hastings.
Elihu S. Rice, 1866.

1. Shall we meet be-yond the riv-er, Where the sur-ges cease to roll?
2. Shall we meet in that blest har-bor, When our storm-y voyage is o'er
3. Shall we meet in yon-der ci-ty, Where the tow'rs of crys-tal shine?
4. Shall we meet with Christ, our Sav-iour, When He comes to claim His own?

Where, in all the bright for-ev-er, Sor-row ne'er shall press the soul?
Shall we meet and cast the an-chor By the fair ce-les-tial shore?
Where the walls are all of jas-per, Built by work-man-ship di-vine?
Shall we know His bless-ed fa-vor, And sit down up-on His throne?

Cho.—Shall we meet, shall we meet, Shall we meet be-yond the riv-er?

Shall we meet be-yond the riv-er, Where the sur-ges cease to roll?

WHILE THE MORNING BELLS ARE RINGING.

"Sicilian Hymn."

1. While the morn-ing bells are ring-ing, We to Thee our songs would raise,
2. When the night was fold-ed o'er us, Heav-y dark-ness shut us in;
3. Thanks to Thee, O heaven-ly Fath-er, For Thine all-pro-tect-ing arm;

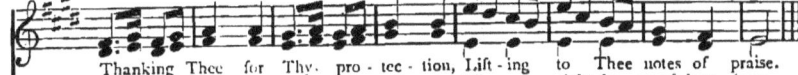

Thanking Thee for Thy pro-tec-tion, Lift-ing to Thee notes of praise.
But we slept in peace-ful qui-et, Thou our night-ly guard hast been.
Thro' the day, we pray thee, keep us Free from e-vil, safe from harm.

DOXOLOGY.

May the grace of Christ, our Saviour,
And the Father's boundless love,
With the Holy Spirit's favor,
Rest upon us from above!

Thus may we abide in union
With each other and the Lord,
And possess, in sweet communion,
Joys that earth can ne'er afford.

BEAUTIFUL SPRING-TIME.

Expression.

1. Beau - ti - ful   Spring-time! bright, blooming   ro - ses, When hope with   pleas - ure
2. Beau - ti - ful   Spring-time! sea - son de - part - ed, When birds were   sing - ing

sweet - ly   re - po - ses, Dream-ing of   glad - ness when day - light   clo - ses,
gay   and light - heart - ed, Tell - ing of   joys when our ear - ly   life   start - ed,

Dreams of the heart when no sor - row was near,   Oh! hap - py days! we can nev - er for -
Oh! how those mo - ments have fad-ed   a - way!   Oh! blissful hours! we shall ev - er re -

·   get   thee, Life was too sweet, ev - 'ry moment was dear! We wandered at even-ing o'er
mem - ber: Sweet was our young   life—too sweet to de - cay! We hear the bells chim-ing, when

val - ley and foun-tain, Thro' for-est and dell,   by the swift-gliding stream: We roamed with light
peaceful - ly dreaming Of   past hap-py hours— of our loved happy band; Tho' Time spreads his

step to the   mur-mur-ing foun-tain, 'Twas long, long a - go,   but it seems a sweet
pin - ions with   ra - di - ant seem-ing, He leads us at last   to the beau - ti - ful

dream, Sweet dream, sweet dream, beau - ti - ful dream, Sweet dream, sweet dream,
land! Bright land, bright land, beau - ti - ful land, Bright land, bright land,

beau - ti - ful dream, Beau - ti - ful dream, beau - ti - ful dream.
beau - ti - ful land, Beau - ti - ful land, beau - ti - ful land.

OH, COULD OUR THOUGHTS.

GERMAN.
ANNE STEELE, 1764.

1. Oh, could our thoughts and wish - es fly A - bove these gloom-y shades, To
2. Lord, send a beam of light di - vine, To guide our up - ward aim! With

those bright worlds beyond the sky, Which sor - row ne'er in - vades! There joys, un-seen by
one re - viv - ing touch of Thine, Our lan - guid hearts inflame, Then shall, on faith's sub-

mor - tal eyes, Or reason's fee - ble ray, In ev - er-blooming prospect rise, Un-
lim - est wing, Our ardent wishes rise To those bright scenes where pleasures spring, Im-

con - scious of de - cay, Un - con - scious of de - cay.
mor - tal in the skies, Im - mor - tal in the skies.

THRO' the Dark Ages music was kept alive mainly by tradition. In the churches its religious element preserved it, while the minne-singers and troubadours, singing of rare knightly deeds, made it an essential accomplishment for those who sought welcome in courts and palaces. Yet to the meister-singers rather than the minne-singers do we owe that which was best worth preserving, the popular element in music, since a language, an art, a religion, to live, must have its abiding-place, its shrine, among the homes and in the hearts of the people. The guilds of the meister-singers were established in the chief cities of Germany, Nuremberg the chief, and chiefest in Nuremberg was Hans Sachs, the shoe-maker, whose name is famous the world over, even without Herr Wagner's opera of *Die Meistersinger*. Those who have seen Kaulbach's cartoon of the "Era of the Reformation" will recall with pleasure the strong, earnest face of the musical cobbler, with whom Luther himself must share some of his glory. The resistless weight and influence of these guilds came from their genuine democracy. Numbering neither knights nor nobles in their ranks, but recruited from the burghers, tradesmen, craftsmen, and plain citizens, they brought com-

WHILE THE DAYS ARE GOING BY.

A. NETTLETON.

1. There are lone-ly hearts to cher-ish, While the days are go-ing by;
2. There's no time for i-dle scorn-ing, While the days are go-ing by;
2. All the lov-ing links that bind us While the days are go-ing by;

There are wea-ry souls that per-ish, While the days are go-ing by;
Let my face be like the morn-ing, While the days are go-ing by;
One by one we leave be-hind us, While the days are go-ing by;

If a smile we can re-new, As our jour-ney we pur-sue,
Oh! the world is full of sighs, Full of sad and weep-ing eyes,
But the seeds of good we sow, Both in shade and sun will grow,

Oh, the good we all may do, While the days are go-ing by!
Help your fal-len broth-ers rise, While the days are go-ing by!
And will keep our hearts a-glow, While the days are go-ing by!

mon-sense in close contact with learning; they sang at the workshop and the forge, at the cobbler's bench and at the loom. Not alone in church, but at home and abroad, music was a bond of union, interwoven with their religious aspirations; it was also their recreation, with a good share of hard, earnest work and careful training, in obedience to strict rules and regulations, under skillful leaders, to make their music possible. It was these meistersingers which made Germany a musical people, ready for Luther's hymns, to which, indeed, music gave wings, doing more than even the great reformer's preaching for the spread of Gospel truth: so simple and effective are some of the great agents of God. Music had at last become the people's possession; not alone a source of enjoyment and gratification to the refined and cultivated, but a mighty means for a mighty end, for the civilization and improvement of all classes—a leaven wherewith to leaven and lift the whole world. From the hour that music ceased to be the exclusive possession of musicians, like religion when it passed from the hands of monks and priests, its power became infinite.—*Gray.*

I'LL DO MY DUTY.

Earnestly.

SONGS OF GLADNESS.

1. Though the clouds are low'r - ing round me, Though the storm - wind blow,
2. If with stern re - buke he chide me, And my spir - it chill,
3. While the hail - stones cold are fall - ing, Pelt - ing on my brow,
4. Saint - ed souls en - throned in glo - ry Passed a - long this way;

Un - be - liev - ing fears con - found me, On - ward still I'll go.
In the Rock - clefts I will hide me, And a - wait his will.
"Fear thou not!" I hear him call - ing, "I am with thee now."
Bonds and fire and scourg - ings go - ry, Filled up all their day.

CHORUS.

By his help I'll do my du - ty, Ev - er trust - ing in his word;

rit.

All my care, and ev' - ry bur - den, Cast - ing on the might - y Lord.

GOD OF OUR FATHERS.

L. MASON, 1832. "DOWNS."

1. God of our fa - thers, by whose hand Thy peo - ple still are blest;
2. Thro' each per - plex - ing path of life Our wand'ring foot - steps guide;
3. Oh, spread thy shelt - 'ring wings a - round, Till all our wand - 'rings cease;

Be with us through our pil - grim - age, Con - duct us to our rest.
Give us each day our dai - ly bread, And rai - ment fit pro - vide.
And at our Fa - ther's loved a - bode, Our souls ar - rive in peace.

MEMORY BELLS.—On the fifth day of my journey across the Syrian desert the air above lay dead, and all the whole earth that I could reach with my utmost sight and keenest listening was still and lifeless as some dispeopled and forgotten world that rolls round and round in the heavens through wasted floods of light. The sun, growing fiercer, shone down more mightily now than ever on me he shone before, and as I drooped my head under his fire and, closing my eyes against the glare that surrounded me, slowly fell asleep, for how many minutes or moments, I cannot tell, but after awhile I was gently awakened by a peal of church bells—my native bells—the innocent bells of Marlen, that never before sent forth their music beyond the Blaygon hills! My first idea naturally was, that I still remained fast under the power of a dream. I roused myself, and drew aside the silk that covered my eyes, and plunged my bare face into the light. Then at least I was well enough wakened, but still those old Marlen bells rang on, not ringing for joy, but properly,

LOVE AND MIRTH.

J. STRAUSS.
BADEN POLKA.

Allegretto.

1. What song doth the crick-et sing? What news doth the swal-low bring?
2. Mark the morn when first she springs Up-ward on her gold-en wings;
3. With the leaves the ap-ples wres-tle, In the grass the dai-sies nes-tle,
2. Is it mirth? then why will man Mar the sweet song all he can?

What doth laughing child-hood tell? What calls out the marriage bell?
Hark! the soar-ing, soar-ing lark, And the echo-ing for-est—hark!
And the sun smiles on the wall, Tell us, What's the cause of all?
Bid him rath-er aye re-joice, With a kind and mer-ry voice,

What say all? "Love and mirth, In the air and in the earth;
What say they? "Love and mirth, In the air and in the earth;
"Mirth and love, Love and mirth, In the air and in the earth;
Bid him sing, "Love and mirth, In the air and in the earth;

Ver-y, ver-y soft and mer-ry is the glad-some song of earth."

prosily, steadily, merrily ringing for "church." After a while the sound died away slowly; it happened that neither I nor any of my party had a watch by which to measure the exact time of its lasting, but it seemed to me that about ten minutes had passed before the bells ceased. I attributed the effect to the great heat of the sun, the perfect dryness of the clear air through which I moved, and the deep stillness of all around me; it seemed to me that these causes, by occasioning a great tension, and consequent susceptibility of the hearing organs, had rendered them liable to tingle under the passing touch of some mere memory, that must have swept across my brain in a moment of sleep. Since my return to England, it has been told me that like sounds have been heard at sea, and that a sailor becalmed under a vertical sun, in the midst of the wide ocean, has listened in trembling wonder to the chime of his own village bells—*Kinglake's Eothen.*

BROTHER SO FINE.

(BRÜDERLEIN FEIN.)

J. DRECHSLER.

Andantino.

1. Broth - er so fine, broth - er so gay, Come, do not be an-gry, I pray, Broth - er so fine,
2. Broth - er so fine, broth - er so gay, Come, do not be an-gry, I pray, Broth - er so fine,
3. Broth - er so fine, broth - er so gay, Friends, oh, let us part to - day, Broth - er so fine,

broth-er so gay, Don't be an - gry, pray. Shines the sun nev-er so clear,
broth-er so gay, Don't be an - gry, pray. Ah, for me, you think no thought,
broth-er so gay, "Fare-well," let us say. Some - times think of me as dear,

Sometime must he dis - ap-pear, Brother so fine, broth-er so gay, Don't be an - gry, pray.
When I'm gone, you deem it nought, Brother so fine, brother so gay, Don't be an - gry, pray.
Mock not at my for - tune drear, Brother so fine, broth-er so gay, Hands we clasp to - day.

THE FAIRY RING.

CHILDHOOD SONGS.

Allegretto.

1. Let us laugh, and let us sing, Danc - ing in a mer - ry ring;
2. Like the sea - sons of the year, Round we cir - cle glad - ly here:
3. Har - ry will be Win - ter wild, Lit - tle Char - ley, Au - tumn mild;

We'll be fai - ries on the green, Sport - ing round the fai - ry queen.
I'll be Sum - mer, you'll be Spring, Danc - ing in a fai - ry ring.
Sum - mer, Au - tumn, Win - ter, Spring, Danc - ing in a fai - ry ring.

Spring and Summer glide away,
Autumn comes with tresses gay;
Winter, hand in hand with Spring,
Dancing in a fairy ring.

Faster! faster! round we go,
While our cheeks like roses glow;
Free as birds upon the wing,
Dancing in a fairy ring.

THE HUMAN EAR.—How do the vibrations of the air speak to your brain? First, I want you to notice how beautifully the outside shell of the ear, or *concha*, as it is called, is curved so that any movement of the air coming to it from the front is caught in it and at once reflected into the opening of the ear. When the air-waves from any quarter have passed in at the opening of your ear, they move all the air in the passage which is called the auditory, or hearing, canal. This canal is lined with little hairs to keep out insects and dust, and the wax which collects in it serves the same purpose. But if too much wax collects, it prevents the air from playing well upon the drum, and therefore makes you deaf. Across the end of this canal a membrane, partly called the *tympanum*, is stretched, like the parchment over the head of a drum, and it is this membrane which moves to and fro as the air-waves strike on it. A violent blow on the ear will sometimes break this delicate membrane, or injure it, and therefore it is very wrong to hit a person violently on the ear. On the other side of this membrane, *inside* the ear, there is air, which fills the whole of the inner chamber and the tube which runs down into the throat. Now, as the drum of the ear is driven to and fro by the sound-waves, it naturally moves the air in the cavity behind it, and also sets in motion here three most curious little bones. The first of these bones is fastened to the middle of the drumhead so that it moves to and fro every time this membrane quivers. The head of this bone fits into a hole in the next bone, the anvil, and is fastened to it by muscles, so as to drag it along with it; but, the muscles being elastic, it can draw back a little from the anvil, and thus give it a blow each time it comes back. This anvil is, in its turn, very firmly fixed to the little bone shaped like a

THE BRIGHT, ROSY MORNING.

Allegretto.

1. The bright ro - sy morn-ing Peeps o - ver the hills, With blush - es a -
2. The deer roused be - fore us, A - way seems to fly, And pants to the
3. The day's sport when o - ver, The fire - side all bright But gives the tired

f Chorus.

dorn - ing   The mea-dows and fields.
cho - rus   Of hounds in full cry.   } While the mer-ry, mer-ry, mer-ry horn Calls,
hun - ter   Fresh charms for the night.

"Come, come a - way, A - wake from your slum - bers, And hail the new day."

stirrup at the end of the chain. This stirrup rests upon a curious body, which looks like a snail-shell with tubes coming out of it. This body, which is called the *labyrinth*, is made of bone, but it has two little windows in it, one covered only by a membrane, while the other has the head of the stirrup resting upon it. Now you will readily understand that when the air in the auditory canal shakes the drumhead to and fro, this membrane must drag the hammer, the anvil, and the stirrup. Each time the drum goes in, the hammer will hit the anvil, and drive the stirrup against the little window; every time it goes out it will draw the hammer, the anvil, and the stirrup out again, ready for another blow. Thus the stirrup is always playing upon this little window. Meanwhile, inside the bony labyrinth there is a fluid like water, and along the little passages are very fine hairs, which wave to and fro like reeds; and whenever the stirrup hits at the little window, the fluid moves these hairs to and fro, and they irritate the ends of a nerve, and this nerve carries the message to the brain. There are also some curious little stones called otoliths, lying in some parts of this fluid, and they, by their rolling to and fro, probably keep up the motion and prolong the sound. You must not imagine we have explained here the many intricacies which occur in the ear. We can only hope to give you a faint idea of it, so that you may picture to yourselves the air-waves moving backwards and forward in the canal of your ear, then the tympanum vibrating to and fro. the hammer hitting the anvil, the stirrup knocking at the little window, the fluid waving the fine hairs and rolling the tiny stones, the end of the nerve quivering, and then in some marvelous way (*how* we know not) the brain hearing the message.—*Buckley.*

I DREAMT I DWELT IN MARBLE HALLS.

M. W. BALFE.
From "BOHEMIAN GIRL."

1. I dreamt that I dwelt in mar - ble halls, With vas - sals and serfs at my
2. I dreamt that suit - ors sought my hand; That knights upon bend - ed

side, . . . And of all who as - sem-bled with - in those walls That I was the
knee, . . And with vows no maid - en heart could withstand, They pledg'd their

hope and the pride. . . . I had rich-es too great to count; could boast Of a
faith to me, . . . And I dreamt that one of that no - ble host Can - e

high an - ces - tral name; But I al - so dreamt, which pleas'd me
forth my hand to claim; But I al - so dreamt, which charm'd me

most, That you lov'd me still the same, that you lov'd me, you lov'd me
most, That you lov'd me still the same, that you lov'd me, you lov'd me

still the same, That you lov'd me, you lov'd me still the same.
still the same, That you lov'd me, you lov'd me still the same.

The following tribute to the memory of the late Matthew Arbuckle, whose magic cornet made his name a household word with millions, will doubtless waken a responsive echo in the heart of every one who was privileged to know that brilliant artist and kindly, courteous gentleman: "Half-a-dozen years ago," writes a lady, one of his pupils, "an old cornet hung upon the wall of my home, and it somehow happened that I tried it 'to see how it would go.' By a little persistence I got a tone, and finally became fascinated with the noise I could produce, and, working away as much as the neighborhood would endure without complaints to the police, I got some mastery.

The performance was horrible, of course, but one April day I appeared at Mr. Arbuckle's door in New York, a petitioner for lessons. I remember how kindly he received me; how he gave me courage at once by commending my poor attempt at 'Robin Adair,' so that he could know what I could do and where to begin with me. I remember the next three months of his helpfulness, his patience, his encouragement, his hopefulness; how he put no limit to the 'hour's lesson' we had bargained for, and often entertained and helped me a whole afternoon, sometimes taking his cornet, and, forgetting all the world else, giving me his wonderful rendering of delightful airs and ballads. I re-

COME, CHEERFUL COMPANIONS.

VIVE LA COMPAGNIE.

Lively.

1. Come, cheerful companions, u - nite in our song, Here's to the friends we love!
2. And first, the dear pa-rents who watch o'er our youth, They are the friends we love!
3. Next, think of the ab-sent to all of us dear, They are the friends we love!
4. And here's to the good, and the wise, and the true, They are the friends we love!

May boun-ti-ful Heav-en their sweet lives prolong! Here's to the friends we love!
And next are the teachers who tell us of truth, They are the friends we love!
Oh, would they were with us, we would they were here! They are the friends we love!
Their beau-ti-ful lives are for me and for you, They are the friends we love!

Oh, sym-pa-thy deepens whenev-er we sing; Friendship's the mys-ti-cal word in our ring;

Here's to our friends! Here's to our friends! Here's to the friends we love!

member, too, his comical running to the corner of the room and hiding his face when I had my lesson poorly, and how he would look over his shoulder laughing at me and shouting : 'Try it again,' and when the work was done to his satisfaction, how proud and glad and happy he seemed. He was every inch a gentleman; in every fibre a musician. He gave me music arranged by his own hand; he selected and tested a cornet for me, and all the 'crooks' and 'mutes' and mouthpieces, and every other appliance of a cornetist's outfit, and there was nothing he could do, by instruction and advice, that he left undone. A country girl of fourteen, alone in the great city so far as kindred were concerned,

he bade me welcome to his home. His wife was almost a mother to me, his daughter a friend indeed. I want to say how good he was, how true to his art, how kind, sweet-tempered, big-hearted—a noble man in every thing.

CHRISTOPHER NORTH, a lover of nature, never said a truer or a wiser thing than this, in his Soliloquy on the Seasons : "Turn from the oracles of man, still dim even in their clearest response—to the oracles of God, which are never dark. Bury all your books when you feel the night of skepticism gathering around you; bury them all, powerful though you may have deemed their spell to illuminate the unfathomable; open your Bible, and all the spiritual world will be as bright as the day."

WHISTLE AND HOE.

ANONYMOUS.

1. There's a boy just o - ver the gar - den fence, Who is whistling all through the
2. Not a word of be - moaning his task, I hear; He has scarcely time for a
3. But, then, while you whis- tle be sure that you hoe, For if you are i - dle the

live- long day; And his work is not just a mere pretence, For you see the weeds he has
growl, I know, For his whis - tle sounds so mer-ry and clear, He must find some pleasure in
briers will spread; And to whistle a - lone to the end of the row May do for the weeds but not

cut a -way.
ev - 'ry row. } Whistle and hoe, sing as you go, Shorten the row by the songs you know;
for the bread. }

songs you know.

SONG OF SEVEN.

JEAN INGELOW.

Brightly.

1. There's no dew left on the dai - sies and clo - ver, There's no rain left in
2. I am old, so old, I can write a let - ter, My birth - day lessons are
3. O Moon! in the night I have seen you sail - ing, And shin - ing so round and

heaven; I've said my "sev - en times" o - ver and o - ver, Seven times one are seven.
done; The lambs play always, they know no bet - ter, They are only one times one.
low; You were bright! ah, bright! but your light is fail-ing, You are nothing now but a bow.

You Moon, have you done something wrong in
    That God has hidden your face? [heaven,
I hope, if you have, you will soon be forgiven,
    And shine again in your place.

O velvet bee, you're a dusty fellow,
    You've powdered your legs with gold;
O brave marsh marybuds, rich and yellow,
    Give me your money to hold.

O Columbine, open your folded wrapper,
    Where two twin turtle-doves dwell;
O cuckoo-pint, toll me the purple clapper,
    That hangs in your clear green bell.

And show me your nest with the young ones in it;
    I will not steal them away;
I am old! you may trust me, linnet, linnet,
    I am seven times one to-day.

II—F

ACQUAINTANCE WITH PAGANINI.—One of Ole Bull's father's assistants played the flute, and used to receive musical catalogues from Copenhagen. Ole devoured the names, and for the first time saw that of Paganini in connection with his famous twenty-four "Caprices." One evening his father brought home two Italians, the first Ole had ever seen. He was then fourteen years of age, and their talk was a revelation to him. They told him all they knew of Paganini, the very mention of whose name excited him. He afterwards related the story to a friend thus: "I went to my sympathizer and said, 'Dear grandmother, can't I have some of Paganini's music?' 'Don't tell any one,' said the dear old woman, 'but I will try to buy a piece of his for you if you are a good child;' and she did try, and I was wild when I at last had the Paganini music. How difficult it was, but oh, how beautiful! The garden-house was more than ever my refuge, and perhaps the cats, who were my only listeners, were not so frightened at my attempts as at my earlier efforts to play Fiorillo's 'Studies,' when I really drove them from their food.

SWEET SONG-BIRD.

J. L. MOLLOY.

On a Tuesday quartet evening, a favorite concerto of Spohr's lay on the leader's stand, and while the company were at supper I tried the score. Carried away with the music, I forgot myself, and was discovered by Lundholm on his return, and scolded for my presumption. 'What impudence! Perhaps you think you could play this at sight, boy!' 'Yes, I think I could.' And as I thought so, I don't know why I should not have said so, do you? The rest of the company had now joined us, and insisted that I should try it. I played the allegro. All applauded save the leader, who looked angry. 'You think you can play anything, then?' he asked, and taking a caprice of Paganini's from the stand, he said: 'Try this.' Now it happened that this very caprice was my favorite, as the cats well knew. I could play it by heart, and I polished it off. When I had finished they all shouted, and, instead of raving, as I thought he would, Lundholm was more polite and kind than he had ever been before, and told me that with very diligent practice I might hope to equal himself some day."—*Ole Bull, a Memoir*

CONGREGATIONAL singing will never become at all general or permanent until the churches employ tunes which have melodies that cling to the memory and touch the feelings or the imagination. Music is not simply a vehicle for carrying a hymn. It is something in itself. No tune is fit to be sung to a hymn which would not be pleasant, in itself, without any words. Any other view of the function of music, if it shall prevail, will in the end bring music to such a tame and tasteless state that a reaction will be inevitable, and the public mind will go to the op-posite extreme. Thus, those who are conscientiously anxious to make music a means of religious feeling, will, by an injudicious method, produce by and by the very mischief which they sought to cure. A corruption of hymns will not be more fatal to public worship than will be a corruption of music. And any theory that denies to church music a power upon the imagination and the feelings, *as music*, and makes it a mere servile attendant upon words, will carry certain mischief upon its path, and put back indefinitely the cause of church music.—*Beecher.*

THE STYRIAN LAND.

Andantino. (DAS STEIERLAND.)

LUDWIG C. SCYDLER, 1844.

1. From the dis-tant Aar, where the wa-ters rave, To the Wen-dish land where flows the
2. There, in for-ests dark, glad the red fawn strays; On the mount-ain fall the sun's bright

1. *Hoch vom Dachstein an, wo der Aar noch haust, Bis zum Wen-den-land am Bett' der*
2. *Wo im dun-keln Wald froh das Reh-lein springt, Droben auf gar stei-ler Ber-ges-*

Saave, Where the shep-herd-ess from her light heart sings, And the hun-ter brave his ri-fle
rays, While the brook-let clear from the glacier springs And the chamois climbs where bird ne'er

Saav', Wo die Sen-ne-rin fro-he Jod-ler singt und der Jä-ger kühn sein Jagdrohr
höh, Wo das Bäch-lein klar aus den Gletschern rinnt und die Gem-sek limmt am Fel-sen

ritard.

swings.
sings. } All this good-ly land is the Styr-ian land, My be-lov-ed, dear-est, na-tive

schwingt:
rand: } *Dieses schö-ne Land ist der Stei-rer Land, ist mein lie-bes, theu-res Hei-mat*

land, All this good-ly land is the Styrian land, My be-lov-ed, dearest, na-tive land.
land, Die-ses schö-ne Land ist der Stei-rer Land, ist mein lie-bes theures Va-ter-land.

When the Alpine vales with the shout resound,
Mid the chime of bells and songs around
Comes the shepherd lad, all his kine at home,
To his dearest maid, no more to roam.—*Cho.*

Wenn im Thal der Alp die Schal mei ertönt,
Unter Glockenklang und heiterm Lied,
Kommt der Hirtenbub' mit den Küh'n daheim
Abends zu der allerliebsten Maid.—Cho.

THOSE EVENING BELLS.

BELLINI.
THOMAS MOORE.

1. Those evening bells, those even - ing bells! How many a tale their mu - sic tells Of

youth, and home, and that sweet time When last I heard their soothing chime! Those

joy - ous hours are passed a - way, And many a heart that then was gay, With-

in the tomb now dark - ly dwells, And hears no more those even - ing bells, With-

in the tomb now dark - ly dwells, And hears no more those even-ing bells,— And

so 'twill be when I am gone; That tune-ful peal will still ring on, While oth - er bards shall walk these dells, And sing your praise, sweet even-ing bells, While oth - er

bards shall walk these dells, And sing your praise, your praise, sweet evening bells.

FLOAT AWAY.

GERMAN MELODY.

1. Float a - way, float a - way, O'er land and o'er sea!
2. Float a - long, float a - long, Ye white, snow - y throng!
3. Oh, the May! oh, the May! The glad month for me!

Float a - way, float a - way, O'er land and o'er sea!
Float a - long, float a - long, Ye white, snow - y throng!
Oh, the May! oh, the May! The glad month for me!

Dark clouds, stay not hith - er, We wait for fair weath-er,
No long - er ye hov - er The green mea - dows o - ver;
The birds and the flow - ers, The bright-fall - ing show-ers,

Float a - way, float a - way, And wel - come the day!
Float a - way, float a - way, Oh, haste ye a - way!
I'm a - way, I'm a - way, On the wings of the May.

LUTHER, to a certain extent, attempted to imitate the work of King David; and, as the latter used the ancient Egyptian music as a groundwork of his system, so Luther sought out and endeavored to preserve all that seemed to him beautiful in the Catholic service. He was especially anxious that the Evangelical Church should not seem to be the foe of any of the fine arts, but should use and foster them. He says, "I rejoice to let the seventy-ninth Psalm, 'O God, the heathen are come,' be sung as heretofore by one choir after another, ... just as it was in the Popish fasts, for it sounds very devotional." Speaking of his desire to make thorough reforms in the music of the people, he writes to a friend, "I wish after the example of the prophets and ancient fathers of the Church, to make German Psalms for the people—that is to say, sacred hymns—so that the Word of God may dwell among the people by means of song also." It was in this year that the first hymnal, spoken of above, was issued. Its title reads, "Some Christian Songs of Praise and Psalms, made from the pure Word of God, from the holy Scriptures, by several highly learned men, to be sung in the Church, as is already partially the practice in Wittenberg, 1524." The success of these hymns was immediate, and from this time there began a composition, arrangement, and adaptation of chorals which remains unparalleled for fertility and activity. Every pastor seemed to think it part of his duty to arrange or compose at least one hymn to the glory of God, and many gave forth whole collections. Thousands were published even in the early days of the Reformation, and to-day each principality and almost each city has its special collection of psalms and of chorals.—*Elson.*

THE HUNTER'S SONG.

SCHÄFFER.

1. See the sun's first gleam on the mountain stream, Now chant your chorus gay, tra, la, la, la, Come,
2. The chamois fleet we long to meet, With dawn's first blushing ray, tra, la, la, la, With
3. Then at e - ven-tide when the sun doth hide Be - hind yon mountain gray, tra, la, la, la, And

comrades, rouse from sloth - ful dream, With joy - ous hearts view the morning beam, For
smil - ing face and bound - ing feet, We'll seek him in his lone re - treat, So a-
shad - ows veil the land-scape wide, A - down the rock - y steep we'll glide, And

soon we must a - way, For soon we must a - way, tra, la, la, la, For
way to the hills, a - way, So a - way to the hills, a - way, tra, la, la, la, So
hail the close of day, And hail the close of day, tra, la, la, la, And

soon we must a - way, For soon we - must a - way, tra, la, la, la, tra, la, la, la.
away to the hills a - way, So a - way to the hills, a - way, tra, la, la, la, tra, la, la, la.
hail the close of day, And hail the close of day, tra, la, la, la, tra, la, la, la.

THE natural history of music is full of wonders. It is as if the Giver of all good gifts had presided over the creation of this with especial love and tenderness, fencing it round with every possible natural security for its safe development, and planting it among those instincts we have least power to pervert. The sense of *time*, which is music's first law, is alone a marvelous guarantee. It is the first condition of musical being—a natural regularity, which we can only learn to hear transgressed from the pleasurable surprise in which the mind is kept for its return. But the true timist is time all over; see the orchestra conductor, with his little wand, by which he may communicate to hundreds of performers the electric flow of true musical measure, and by which the evanescent vibrations of sound seem knit together for action. And then the readiness with which the memory lends itself to the service of music, is a very marked phenomenon peculiar to this faculty. What a paradox it is, that what the mind receives with most passiveness, it retains with most fidelity—laying up choicest things in musical thought or expression, to be ready at any moment for spontaneous reproduction? For not even the exertion of our will is requisite—a thought, nay, the slightest breath of a hint, is sufficient to set the exquisitely sensitive strings of musical memory vibrating, and the emotions that have lain buried for years will come back with a melody. Pictures, poetry, loves, hatreds, and promises of course, are all more fleeting than *tunes*. There is no such pitiless invoker of the ghosts of the past as one bar of a melody that has been connected with them. No such sigh or sob escapes from the heart, as that in the train of some musical reminiscence.

GUADALQUIVER.

C. NELSON.
CHARLES JEFFREYS.

Allegretto Grazioso.

1. Gua-dal-quiv-er, gen-tle riv-er! O'er the vales of fer-tile Spain, In the
2. Bright as ev-er are thy wa-ters! And I love to look on thee, For thy

sun-shine of thy beau-ty, Like a mon-arch, thou dost reign, On thy
brightness is an em-blem Of re-turn-ing joys to me: Gua-dal-

banks I love to wan-der, In the summer moon-beam's glance, When I - be-ria's dark-eyed
quiv-er, gen-tle riv-er! Thou dost wake the old-en strain, And the songs I sung in

daughters Mingle in the joy-ous dance. Gua-dal-quiv-er, gen-tle riv-er, O'er the
child-hood, Now shall welcome thee a gain, Gua-dal-quiv-er, gen-tle riv-er, O'er the

vales of fer-tile Spain, In the sunshine of thy beau-ty, Like a monarch, thou dost reign.

CHEER, BOYS, CHEER.

H. Russell.
Charles Mackay.

1. Cheer, boys, cheer, no more of i - dle sor - row, Courage! true hearts shall
2. Cheer, boys, cheer, the stead - y breeze is blow - ing, To float us free - ly

bear us on our way; Hope points be - fore and shows the bright to - mor - row;
o'er the o - cean's breast; The world shall fol - low in the track we're go - ing,

Let us for - get the dark - ness of to - day. So fare - well, England,
The star of Em - pire glit - ters in the West. Here we had toil and

much as we a - dore thee, We'll dry the tears that we have shed be - fore;
lit - tle to re - ward it, But there shall plen - ty smile up - on our pain;

Why should we weep to sail in search of for - tune? So fare - well, England! fare -
And ours shall be the prai - rie and the for - est, And bound - less meadows ripe,

well for - ev - er - more. Cheer, boys, cheer for coun - try, moth - er coun - try,
ripe with gol - den grain. Cheer, boys, cheer for England, moth - er Eng - land,

Cheer, boys, cheer the will-ing strong right hand, Cheer, boys, cheer, there's
Cheer, boys, cheer, u-nit-ed heart and hand, Cheer, boys, cheer, there's

wealth for hon-est la-bor, Cheer, boys, cheer for the new and hap-py land!

MAKE YOUR MARK.

Firmly.

1. In the quar-ries should you toil, Make your mark! Make your mark! Do you delve up-
2. Would you seek for treasures rare, Make your mark! Make your mark! Wealth that will with
3. Life is fleet-ing as a shade, Make your mark! Make your mark! Marks of some kind

on the soil, Make your mark! Make your mark! In what-ev-er path you go,
gold com-pare, Make your mark! Make your mark! While the light is in thine eye,
must be made, Make your mark! Make your mark! Make it while the arm is strong,

In what-ev-er place you stand, Mov-ing swift or mov-ing slow, With a firm and
While the bloom is on thy cheek, Ere the toils and cares of life, Make the res-o-
In the gol-den hours of youth, Nev-er, nev-er make it wrong, Make it with the

hon-est hand, Make your mark, Make your mark, Make, make your mark!
lu-tion weak, Make your mark, Make your mark, Make, make your mark!
stamp of truth, Make your mark, Make your mark, Make, make your mark!

How true was the conception of the influence which the "harmony of sweet sounds" exerts over the soul, in the mind of him who said, "I would rather write a nation's ballads than make its laws." How different the law-giver's place in the estimation of the people from that of the bard. To the one they accord reverential respect; to the other a true heart-affection and love, handed down, undiminished by the lapse of centuries, from generation to generation. The one lives in his laws, but what power have they over the heart so long as they allow it to beat freely? The other lives in his songs, and *they* can cause the heart to beat and throb, and the soul to move and surge like the restless waves of the sea. There are few of us whose hearts have not been swayed by the power of national music—stirred by those grand anthems of liberty, the "Star Spangled Banner," and "Hail Columbia,"—few who have not, at some time, noted its effect upon others—the ecstatic rapture of the Frenchman thrilled by the inspiring notes of the "Marseillaise;" the deeper, sterner, joyous pride that wells up in the heart of the German as

OH, TAKE ME BACK TO SWITZERLAND.

TYROLESE AIR,
CAROLINE NORTON.

1. By the dark waves of the roll-ing sea, Where the white-sail'd ships are toss-ing free,
2. I see its hills, I see its streams, Its blue lakes haunt my restless dreams:
3. For months a-long that gloom-y shore, 'Mid sea bird's cry and ocean's roar,

Came a youthful maiden, Pale and sor-row-la-den, With a mournful voice sang she: "Oh,
When the day de-clin-eth, Or the bright sun shineth, Pres-ent still its beau-ty seems. Oh,
Sang that mournful maiden, Pale and sorrow la-den, Then her voice was heard no more. For

take me back to Switz-er-land, My own, my dear, my na-tive land; I'll
take me back to Switz-er-land, Up-on the mountain let me stand, Where
far a-way from Switz-er-land, From home, from friends, from na-tive land, Where

brave all dan-gers of the main, To see my own dear land a-gain.
flow'rs are bright, and skies are clear, For oh! I pine, I per-ish here!"
for-eign wild-flow'rs cold-ly wave, The bro-ken-heart-ed found a grave.

he hears the loved "Wacht am Rhein;" the patriotism which fills the heart of the Highlander as he listens to the well-known "Scots, wha hae wi' Wallace bled." But the influence of music over individuals is still stronger, sweeter, holier. How the heart bowed down with crushing sorrow is comforted and soothed by its holy charm! How, after long wanderings from the innocent paths of youth, the weary, sin-sick soul is recalled to the life of truth by hearing some well-remembered strain—perhaps once sung by a dear angel mother in days gone by. In after-life, when youth's pleasures and hopes have given place to age's cares and disappointments, how remembrances of the past are brought back, like bright pictures, by snatches of songs sung in those gay hours of long ago. Then blessed be music, with all its power of witchery and enchantment! Blessed be its holy mission of carrying us away from the bare, discouraging, realities of our lives back to the pleasure-fields of the past, or forward in anticipation to the glad joys of the future.

LIGHT OF OTHER DAYS.

M. W. BALFE.
Words by ALFRED BUNN.

1. The light of oth - er days is fa - ded, And all their glo - ries
2. The leaf which au - tumn tem-pests with - er, The birds which then take

past, For grief with heav - y wing hath sha - ded The hopes too bright to
wing, When win - ter's winds are past, come hith - er, To wel - come back the

last; The world which morn-ing's man - tle cloud - - - ed, Shines
spring; The ve - ry i - vy on the ru - - in In

forth with pur - er rays, But the heart ne'er feels, in sor - row
gloom full life dis - plays, But the heart a - lone sees no re -

shroud - - ed, The light of oth - er days, But the
new - - ing The light of oth - er days, But the

heart ne'er feels, in sor - row shroud - - ed, The light of oth - er days.
heart a - lone sees no re - new - ing The light of oth - er days.

In 1827, Beethoven was dying. He had heard with surprise that Schubert had composed more than five hundred songs, and spent some of his last hours in reading them (the only way in which they could reach him) over and over, exclaiming, "I too should have set this music." Schubert came with one of the brothers Huttenbrenner, to inquire for the master. Beethoven was lying almost insensible; but as they approached the bed, he appeared to rally for a moment, looked fixedly at them and muttered something unintelligible. Schubert stood gazing at him for some moments in silence and then, suddenly bursting into tears, left the room. On the day of the funeral Schubert and two of his friends were sitting together in a tavern, and, after the German fashion,

they drank to the soul of the great man whom they had so lately borne to the tomb. It was then proposed to drink to that one of them who should be the first to follow the great departed, and hastily filling the cup, Schubert drank to himself.—*Haweis.*

The nature of music is three-fold, like that of a man to whom it appeals. Therefore it may be regarded as a sensuous art, in that it delights the ear; as a psychologic art, in that it records the emotions, and requires mental operations on the part of the hearer for its due appreciation; and, as it involves agreements, differences, symmetries, complexities, with other marked qualities, among them order in apparent disorder, it may be regarded as a branch of science that is closely allied to mathematics.

ROCKED IN THE CRADLE OF THE DEEP.

J. P. Knight.
Emma Willard. 1832.

1. Rock'd in the cra-dle of the deep, I lay me down in peace to sleep. Se-
2. And such the trust that still were mine, Tho' stor-my winds swept o'er the brine, Or

cure I rest up - on the wave, For thou, Oh! Lord, hast pow'r to save. I
tho' the tempest's fie - ry breath Roused me from sleep to wreck and death. In

know thou wilt not slight my call, For thou dost mark the spar - row's fall; And
o - cean cave still safe with Thee, The germ of im - mor - tal - i - ty; And

calm and peaceful is my sleep . . Rock'd in the cra-dle of the deep, And

calm and peace-ful is my sleep, . . Rock'd in the cra - dle of the deep.

I DREAM OF ALL THINGS FREE.

Von Weber.
Felicia Hemans.

Allegro Moderato.

1. I dream of all things free, Of a gal - lant, gal - lant
2. I dream of some proud bird, A bright-eyed moun - tain
3. Of a hap - py for - est child, With the fawns and flowers at

bark, That sweeps thro' storm and sea, Like an ar - row to its
king; In my vis - ions I have heard The rush - ing of his
play; Of an In - dian 'midst the wild, With the stars to guide his

mark; Of a stag that o'er the hills . . . Goes bound-ing in his
wing. I fol - low some wild riv - er . . . On whose breast no sail may
way; Of a chief his war - riors leading; Of an ar - cher's green-wood

glee; Of a thou - sand flash - ing rills; Of all things glad and
be; Dark woods a - round it shiv - er— I dream of all things
tree; My heart in chains is bleed - ing; And I dream of all things

free; Of a thou - sand flash - ing rills; Of all things glad and
free; Dark woods a - round it shiver I dream of all things
free; My heart in chains is bleeding; And I dream of all things

free, Of all things glad and free, glad and free.
free, I dream of all things free, all things free.
free, And I dream of all things free, all things free.

"CHEER thee, my Nymphalin," said the prince of the fairies, "we will lay the tempest;" and he waved his sword and muttered the charms which curb the winds and roll back the marching thunder; but for once the tempest ceased not at his spells; and now, as the fairies sped along the troubled air, a pale and beautiful form met them by the way, and they paused and trembled. For the power of that Shape could vanquish even them. It was the form of a Female, with golden hair, crowned with a chaplet of withered leaves; her bosom, of an exceeding beauty, lay bare to the wind, and an infant was clasped upon it, hushed into a sleep so still that neither the roar of the thunder, nor the livid lightning flashing from cloud to cloud, could even ruffle, much less arouse, the slumberer. And the face of the Female was unutterably calm and sweet (though with a something of severe); there was no line or wrinkle in her hueless brow; care never wrote its defacing characters upon that everlasting beauty. It knew no sorrow or change; ghost-like and shadowy floated on that Shape through the abyss of Time, governing the world with an unquestioned and noiseless sway. And the children of the green solitudes of the earth, the lovely fairies of my tale, shuddered as they gazed and recognized— the form of Death. "And why," said the beautiful Shape, with a voice as soft as the last sighs of a dying babe; "why trouble ye the air with spells? mine

SWITZER'S SONG OF HOME.

IGNATZ MOSCHELES.

```
1. Why   ah   why, my heart, this   sad - ness?      Why   'mid scenes like these de -
2. All   that's dear  to   me   is   want - ing,      Lone  and cheer - less here   I
3. Give   me   those, I   ask  no   oth - er,        Those  that bless the hum - ble

cline?   Where all,  tho' strange, is joy and  glad-ness,    Say,  what wish can yet be
roam;    The  stran - ger's joys, howe'er en - chanting,    To me  can nev - er  be like
dome,    Where dwell my fa - ther and my  moth - er,       Give,  oh, give me back my

thine?   Oh,   say,   what wish can  yet   be  thine?
home,    To    me    can  nev - er   be  like  home.
home,    My    own,   my  dear, my  na - tive  home.
```

is the hour and the empire, and the storm is the creature of my power. Far yonder to the west it sweeps over the sea, and the sea ceases to vex the waves; it smites the forest, and the destined tree, torn from its roots, feels the winter strip the gladness from its boughs no more! The roar of the elements is the herald of eternal stillness to their victims; and they who hear the progress of my power idly shudder at the coming of peace. And thou, O tender daughter of the fairy king! why grievest thou at a mortal's doom? Knowest thou not that sorrow cometh with years, and that to live is to mourn? Blessed is the flower that, nipped in its early spring, feels not the blasts that, one by one, scatter its blossoms around it, and leave but the barren stem. Blessed are the young whom I clasp to my breast, and lull into the sleep which the storm cannot break, nor the morrow arouse to sorrow or to toil. The heart that is stilled in the bloom of its first emotions,—that turns with its last throb to the eye of love, as yet unlearned in the possibility of change,—has exhausted already the wine of life, and is saved only from the lees. As the mother soothes to sleep the wail of her troubled child, I open my arms to the vexed spirit, and my bosom cradles the unquiet to repose!"—The fairies answered not, for a chill and a fear lay over them, and the Shape glided on; ever as it passed away through the veiling clouds they heard its low voice singing amidst the roar of the storm, as the dirge of the water-sprite over the vessel it hath lured into the whirlpool or the shoals.—*Bulwer.*

BEETHOVEN'S forte was extempore playing, which must have been extraordinary from what is said of its effects; but he was entirely destitute of the coolness and self-possession necessary for the accurate rendering of written music, and probably his published works have been played by others with much more effect than he usually gave them himself. It was the same with his conducting of the orchestra, in which even before his deafness, he often confused the players rather than assisted them. One story is told which conveys some idea of his want of presence of mind under such circumstances. He was in the habit, when conducting, of expressing a loud passage by throwing his arms up, or out, at full stretch.

When playing one of his own concertos, during a long passage for the band where the piano was silent, he forgot his position, and fancying he was conducting, threw his arms out at a certain loud chord, and knocked both candles off the piano, and when they were picked up and the passage repeated, by the time the same chord recurred he had forgotten the accident and did the same again. The audience, with all their respect for him, were, naturally enough, convulsed with laughter, which so irritated him that at the next solo he broke several strings of the piano. When to this nervous excitability was added his lamentable affliction, deafness, it is no wonder that at last his friends persuaded him to relinquish the task.

THE CARRIER DOVE.

D. JOHNSON.

1. Fly a-way to my na-tive land, sweet dove! Fly a-way to my na-tive land, And bear these lines to my la-dy love, That I've traced with a fee-ble hand. She mar-vels much at my long de-lay, A ru-mor of death she has heard, Or she thinks, per-haps, I false-ly stray,—Then fly to her bower, sweet bird.

2. Oh! fly to her bower, and say the chain Of the ty-rant is o-ver me now, That I nev-er shall mount my steed a-gain, With hel-met up-on my brow; No friend to my lat-tice a sol-ace brings, Ex-cept when your voice is heard, When you beat the bars With your snow-y wings—Then fly to her bower, sweet bird.

3. I shall miss thy vis-it at dawn, sweet dove! I shall miss thy vis-it at eve! But bring me a line from my la-dy love, And then I shall cease to grieve! I can bear in a dun-geon to waste away youth; I can fall by the con-queror's sword; But I cannot en-dure She should doubt my truth—Then fly to her bower, sweet bird.

MANY a turbulent outbreak among little folks has been quelled by starting a bright, merry chorus, whose joyous rhythm proves a safe outlet for that restlessness which, rather than depravity, is the cause of nine-tenths of childhood's misdemeanors. Nor are we children of a larger growth less amenable to the power of united song in bringing harmony out of discord, and rest and refreshment to wearied body and disheartened soul. "When the battle of Leuthen had been fought, and the victors, fatigued almost to death, were sinking down in the chilling rain among the slain that lay scattered on the bloody field, then, in the darkness of the night, a single voice broke forth with the old choral, 'Nun danket alle Gott!' Soon a second voice joined, then a third, and so more and more, until the whole army took up the hymn; and thus the simple song—in which the feeling of patriotism and military glory, united with the consciousness of a great deed accomplished and of pious gratitude toward the mighty Ruler of Battles—inspired their hearts with new life, and strengthened them to follow up the victory so nobly won."

I LOVE TO TELL THE STORY.

KATE HANKEY.
WM. G. FISCHER, by per.

1. I love to tell the sto - ry Of un - seen things a - bove, Of Je - sus and his
2. I love to tell the sto - ry; More won - der-ful it seems Than all the gold-en
3. I love to tell the sto - ry; 'Tis pleas - ant to re - peat What seems each time I
4. I love to tell the sto - ry; For those who know it best, Seem hun - ger-ing and

glo - ry, Of Je - sus and his love; I love to tell the sto - ry, Be-
fan - cies Of all our gold-en dreams. I love to tell the sto - ry, It
tell it, More won - der - ful - ly sweet. I love to tell the sto - ry, For
thirst-ing To hear it like the rest. And when, in scenes of glo - ry, I

cause I know 'tis true; It sat - is - fies my long-ings As noth-ing else can do.
did so much for me! And that is just the rea - son I tell it now to thee.
some have nev-er heard The mes-sage of sal - va - tion From God's own ho - ly word.
sing the new, new song, 'Twill be the old, old sto - ry That I have loved so long.

Chorus.

I love to tell the sto - ry, 'Twill be my theme in glo - ry,

To tell the old, old sto - ry, Of Je - sus and his love.

WHERE ARE THE FRIENDS OF MY YOUTH?

George Barker.

1. Where are the friends of my youth? Say, where are those cherish'd ones gone? And why have they dropped with the leaf, Ah! why have they left me to mourn? Their voi-ces still sound in mine ear, Their fea-tures I see in my dreams, And the world is a wil-der-ness drear, As a wide-spreading des-ert, it seems. Ah! . . . . . where are the friends of my youth, Ah! where are those cherish'd ones gone? And why have they dropped with the leaf, Ah! why have they left me to mourn?

2. Say, can I ev-er a-gain, Such ties can I ev-er re-new? Or feel those warm pul-ses a-gain, Which beat for the dear ones I knew? The world as a win-ter is cold, Each charm seems to van-ish a-way, My heart is now blighted and old, It shares in all Na-ture's de-cay. Ah! . . . . . where are the friends of my youth, Say, where are those cherish'd ones gone? And why have they dropped with the leaf, Ah! why have they left me to mourn?

II—G

SONG OF THE BROOK.

ALFRED TENNYSON.
"SHEPHERD BOY," by G. D. WILSON.

mf

1. I come from haunts of coot and hern, I make a sud-den sal-ly And
2. I steal by lawns and grass-y plots, I slide by ha-zel cov-ers; I
3. I wind a-bout, and in and out, With here a blos-som sail-ing, And

spark-le out a-mong the fern, To bick-er down a val-ley, By
move the sweet for-get-me-nots That bloom for hap-py lov-ers, With
here and there a lust-y trout, And here and there a grey-ling, And

thir-ty hills I hur-ry down, Or slip be-tween the rid-ges, By
many a curve my banks I fret, By many a field and fal-low, And
here and there a foam-y flake, Up-on me, as I trav-el, With

a tempo..

twen-ty thorps, a lit-tle town, And half a hun-dred bridg-es, Till
many a fair-y fore-land set With wil-low weed and mal-low, I
many a sil-v'ry wa-ter-break A-bove the gold-en grav-el; And

last by Phil-ip's farm I flow, To join the brim-ming riv-er, For
chat-ter, chat-ter, as I flow, To join the brim-ming riv-er, For
draw them all a-long, and flow, To join the brim-ming riv-er, For

men may come and men may go, But I go on for - ev - er. And

cres. *ril.*

in and out I curve and flow, To join the brim - ming riv - er, For

men may come and men may go, But I go on for - ev - er, For

men may come and men may go, But I go on for - ev - er.

THE LIFE LAID DOWN.

James Langran

1. Wea - ry of earth, and la - den with my sin, I look to Heav'n and long to en - ter in;
2. It is the voice of Je - sus that I hear, His are the hands stretched out to draw me near,

But there no e - vil thing may find a home; And yet I hear a voice that bids me "Come."
And His the blood that can for all a - tone, And set me faultless there before the throne.

'Twas He who found me on the deathly wild,
And made me heir of Heaven, the Father's child;
And day by day, whereby my soul may live,
Gives me His grace of pardon, and will give.

Yea, Thou will answer for me, righteous Lord:
Thine all the merits, mine the great reward;
Thine the sharp thorns, and mine the golden crown,
Mine the life won, and Thine the life laid down.

THE skill of the painter and sculptor, which comes in aid of the memory and imagination, is, in its highest degree, one of the rarest, as it is one of the most exquisite, accomplishments within our attainment. In its perfection it is as seldom witnessed as in speech or music. The plastic hand must be moved by the same ethereal instinct as the eloquent lips or the recording pen. The number of those who can discern the finished statue in the heart of the shapeless block, and bid it start into artistic life— who are endowed with the exquisite gift of moulding the rigid bronze or the lifeless marble into graceful, majestic, and expressive forms—is not greater than the number of those who are able with equal majesty, grace and expressiveness to make the spiritual essence, the finest shades of thought and feeling, sensible to the mind through the eye and the ear in the mysterious embodiment of the written and the spoken word. If Athens in her palmiest days had but one Pericles, she had also but one Phidias.—*Everett.*

OVER THERE.

D. W. C. HUNTINGTON.
T. C. O'KANE, by per.

1. Oh, think of a home o - ver there, By the side of the riv - er of light, Where the saints all im-mor - tal and fair, Are robed in their gar - ments of white.

2. Oh, think of the friends o - ver there, Who be - fore us the jour - ney have trod, Of the songs that they breathe on the air, In their home in the pal - ace of God.

3. I'll soon be at home o - ver there, For the end of my jour - ney I see; Ma - ny dear to my heart o - ver there, Are watch - ing and wait - ing for me.

Chorus.

O - ver there, o - ver there, o - ver there, o - ver there, Oh, think of a home o - ver there, o - ver there; O - ver there, o - ver there, o - ver there, o - ver there, Oh, think of a home o - ver there.

BUT THE LORD IS MINDFUL OF HIS OWN.

MENDELSSOHN.
From "ST. PAUL."

Andantino.

But the Lord is mindful of his own, He re - members his chil - dren, But the

ritard.

Lord is mindful of his own, the Lord remembers his chil-dren, re - mem - bers his

chil - dren, Bow down before Him, ye might - y, for the Lord is near us!

cres.

Bow down before Him, ye migh-ty, for the Lord is near us! yea, the

Lord is mind-ful of his own; He re - members his chil - dren; Bow down be-

cres.

fore Him, ye might-y, for the Lord is near us!

As a nation we are not yet a musical people in the sense in which Germany and Italy are musical, but there is a decided movement among the people which is a sign of promise. The best and most encouraging indication is that music is no longer regarded as simply an accomplishment. Like the Greeks, we are realizing the necessity of æsthetic culture if we would have our young men and young women developed into well-rounded, harmonious characters. Far more than in those older lands do we need the universal art, which, while it crowns all others, may yet precede all others. In this new land there are, there can be, no wonders of architecture sacred with age and hallowed memories. Here are no galleries of sculpture and painting. They are the growth of an older civilization, of a repose and patience as far as possible opposed to our restless, unceasing activity of brain and body. De Staël calls architecture "frozen music." As truly may we call music "living, breathing architecture." Governed by as perfect laws of harmony and proportion, it has, besides, a principle of life which even architecture, painting, or sculpture can not have. A perfect completed poem that lacks no touch from the master-hand that created it, a wonder of harmony and melody so perfect in form and beauty that a note added or withdrawn would mar its loveliness, may live anew, be anew created by the genius of the interpreter. It is infinite in its meaning, infinite in its suggestions, infinite in its glimpses of heavenly truth and beauty.—*Gray.*

IF THOU WERT BY MY SIDE.

S. NELSON.
REGINALD HEBER.

1. If thou wert by my side, my love, How fast would eve-ning fail, In green Ben-gal-a's palm-y grove, List-'ning the night-in-gale. If thou, my love, wert by my side, My ba-bies at my knee, How gai-ly would our pin-nace glide O'er Gun-ga's mi-mic sea.

2. I miss thee at the dawn-ing gray, When, on our deck re-clined, In care-less ease my limbs I lay, And woo the cool-er wind. I miss thee, when by Gun-ga's stream My twi-light steps I guide; But most be-neath the lamp's pale beam, I miss thee from my side!

3. I spread my books, my pen-cil try, The lin-g'ring noon to cheer; But miss thy kind ap-prov-ing eye, Thy meek at-ten-tive ear, But when of morn and eve the star gleam bright, they say, Be-holds me on my knee; But feel, though thou art dis-tant far, Thy pray'rs as-cend for me.

4. Then on, then on where du-ty leads, My course be on-ward still; O'er broad Hin-dos-tan's sul-try meads, O'er bleak Al-mo-ra's hill. Thy towers, Bom-bay, gleam bright, they say, A-cross the dark blue sea; But ne'er were hearts so light and gay As soon shall meet in thee.

THE BRAVE OLD OAK.

E. J. Loder.
H. F. Chorley.

Maestoso.

1. A song for the oak, the brave old oak, Who hath ruled in the greenwood long, Here's
2. He saw the rare times, when the Christmas chimes Were a mer - ry sound to hear, And the

health and re-nown to his broad green crown, And his fif - ty arms so strong.
squire's wide hall, and the cot - tage small, Were full of Christmas cheer.

There is fear in his frown when the sun goes down, And the fire in the west fades out; And he
And all the day to the re - beck gay, They carol'd with gladsome swains. They are

show - eth his might on a wild midnight, When the storms through his branches shout. Then
gone, they are dead, in the church-yard laid, But the brave tree, he still re - mains. Then

sing to the oak, the brave old oak, Who hath stood in his pride so long; And

still flour - ish he, a hale green tree, When a hun - dred years are gone.

TRAINING.—The feeblest attempt in the smallest, most obscure Western village to advance true art has weight and influence, and is not lost though it seems too insignificant to be noted. If all were generals, we should have no army. The smallest drummer-boy at the farthest outpost of our civilization is an essential part of the whole, helping and advancing the good cause by his earnestness and fidelity, inspiring some faint, feeble heart to one more effort, passing on the good word of obedience, in the faith that ten times one is ten, till the tens are hundreds, the hundreds thousands, the thousands a multitude that no man can number. If even a feeble effort is of value, how much more valuable is a well-directed, intelligent effort of one who has been systematically trained, who sees the end from the beginning, and, sure of his ground, strengthened by sympathy and that sense of communion which is the very life of the soul, works intelligently for a definite end! For this a thorough, careful training is needed—a training which, in its elementary condition, should precede any question of talent or special ability. We do not ask children if they have a predilection for the alphabet or the multiplication table; it is their

COLUMBIA, GOD PRESERVE THEE FREE!

JOSEPH HAYDN.

1. Ark of Free-dom! Glo-ry's dwelling! Columbia, God pre-serve thee free! When the
2. Land of high, he - ro - ic glo - ry: Land whose touch bids slav'ry flee: Land whose
3. Vain - ly 'gainst thine arm con - tend-ing, Ty - rants know thy might, and flee. Free - dom's

storms are round thee swelling, Let thy heart be strong in thee, God is with thee, wrong re-
name is writ in sto - ry, Rock and ref - uge of the free: Ours thy greatness—ours thy
cause on earth de - fend-ing, Man has set his hope on thee; Widening glo - ry—peace un -

pell-ing: He a - lone thy champion be.
glo - ry; We will e'er be true to thee. } Ark of Free-dom! Glory's dwelling! Columbia,
end-ing—Thy re-ward and por-tion be.

God preserve thee free! Ark of Freedom! Glory's dwelling! Columbia, God preserve thee free!

right; they are to have it whether they specially desire it or not. All will not become Newtons or Shakespeares; but without the preliminary training they have no possibility of appreciating either the one or the other. The receivers must outnumber givers in any one direction; there must be audience as well as orator. The better trained the audience, the better oratory will they demand and receive. As simple, as unquestioning, should be the first part of a child's musical education, till, unconsciously, the page of music is as expressive and intelligible to him as a page of printing, remembering always that to vocalize a scale is much easier than to learn the different sounds in the alphabet, a far simpler task to master in childhood than in maturer years. Vocal music, which at first is largely imitative, is the easiest method for very young children, who, experience proves, will learn good music much more readily than bad, and are swayed and influenced beyond computation by the sentiment of the hymns and songs learned at school and sung in unison, or by the sort of musical atmosphere in which they find themselves at home.

HAIL TO THE CHIEF.

Sanderson.
Sir Walter Scott.

Maestoso.

1. Hail to the chief, who in tri - umph advan-ces, Honor'd and blessed be the ever-green pine!
2. Ours is no sapling, chance-sown by the fountain, Blooming at Beltane, in winter to fade; When the
3. Row, vassals, row, for the pride of the Highlands! Stretch to your oars for the evergreen pine!

Long may the tree in his ban - ner that glances, Flour-ish, the shel-ter and grace of our line.
whirl-wind has stripp'd ev'ry leaf on the mountain, The more shall Clan-Alpine exult in her shade.
Oh, that the rosebud that graces yon islands, Were wreath'd in a gar-land a-round him to twine!

Hail to the chief, who in tri - umph ad-van-ces, Honor'd and bless'd be the ever-green pine!
Ours is no sapling, chance-sown by the fountain, Blooming at Beltane, in winter to fade; When the
Row, vassals, row, for the pride of the Highlands! Stretch to your oars for the evergreen pine!

Long may the tree in his ban-ner that glances, Flour-ish, the shel - ter and grace of our line.
whirl-wind has stripp'd ev'ry leaf on the mountain, The more shall Clan-Alpine exult in her shade.
Oh, that the rose-bud that graces yon islands, Were wreath'd in a garland around him to twine!

Allegro.

Heav'n send it happy dew, Earth lend it sap a-new; Gai-ly to bourgeon and broad-ly to grow;
Moor'd in the rift-ed rock, Proof to the tempest shock, Firmer he roots him, the ruder it blow;
O that some seedling gem, Worthy such noble stem, Honor'd and bless'd in their shadow might grow!

While ev'ry highland glen, Sends our shout back again, "Roderigh Vich Alpine dhu, ho! i-e-roe!"
Menteith and Breadalbane, then, Echo his praise again, "Roderigh Vich Alpine dhu, ho! i-e-roe!"
Loud should Clan-Alpine then, Ring from her deepmost glen, "Roderigh Vich Alpine dhu, ho! ieroe!
(Roder-ik Vik Alpen du, ho! i-e-ro.)

LOVE SONGS.—This is one and a chief charm of Burns' love-songs, that they are certainly of all love-songs except those wild snatches left to us by her who flung herself from the Leucadian rock the most in earnest, the tenderest, the "most moving, delicate and full of life." Burns makes you feel the reality and the depth, the truth of his passion; it is not her eye-lashes, or her nose, or her dimple, that are "winging the fervor of his love;" not even her soul; it is herself. This concentration and earnestness, this *perfervor* of

our Scottish love poetry, seems to me to contrast curiously with the light, trifling philandering of the English; indeed, as far as I remember, we have almost no love-songs in English of the same class as those of Burns. They are mostly of the genteel, or of the nautical (some of these capital), or of the comic school. Do you know, "Oh, wert thou in the cauld blast?" the most perfect, the finest love-song in our or in any language; the love being affectionate more than passionate, love in possession not in pursuit. The follow-

THY NAME WAS ONCE THE MAGIC SPELL.

A. COWELL.
CAROLINE NORTON.

1. Thy name was once the ma-gic spell By which my heart was bound, And burn-ing dreams of light and love, Were wa-kened by that sound, My heart beat quick, when stran-ger tongues With i-dle praise or blame A- woke its deep-est thrill of life, To trem-ble at thy name.

2. Long years, long years have passed a-way And al-tered is thy brow, And we who met so fond-ly once, Must meet as stran-gers now; The friends of yore come round me still, But talk no more of thee; 'Tis i-dle e'en to wish it now— For what art thou to me!

3. Yet still thy name, thy blessed name, My lone-ly bos-om fills, Like ech-o that hath lost it-self A-mong the dis-tant hills: The still with mel-an-cho-ly note, Keeps faint-ly ling'-ring on, When the joy-ous sound that woke it first, Is gone, for-ev-er gone.

ing is Mr. Chambers' account of the origin of this song: Jessy Lewars had a call one morning from Burns. He offered, if she would play him any tune of which she was fond, and for which she desired new verses, that he would do his best to gratify her wish. She at once sat down at the piano, and played over and over the air of an old song beginning with the words, "The robin cam' to the wren's nest." . . . Love never faileth; but whether there be prophecies, they shall

fail; whether there be tongues, they shall cease; whether there be knowledge, it shall vanish away; but love is of God, and cannot fail.—*Dr. John Brown.*

HOME was always a mellow Saxon word; but it rings sweeter than ever now-a-days, thanks to Payne's immortal song. When we are told that charitable men have erected an orphans' home, an outcasts' home, a sailors' home, etc., all this, indeed, wins the English ear and warms the English heart.

MORE than 2,000 years ago, Plato, the propounder of a system of ethics second only to Christianity, said of music: "To look upon music as a mere amusement cannot be justified. Music which has no other aim can neither be considered of value nor viewed with reverence." And these words are re-echoed in our day by England's great philanthropist and statesman, W. E. Gladstone, when he said: "They who think music ranks among the trifles of existence are in gross error, because from the beginning of the world down to the present time, it has been one of the most forcible instruments both for training, for arousing, and for governing the mind and the spirit of man. There was a time when letters and civilization had but begun to dawn upon the world. In that day music was not unknown. On the contrary, it was so far from being a mere servant and handmaid of common and light amusement, that the great and noble art of poetry was essentially wedded to that of music, so that there was no poet who was not a musician; there was no verse

THE PEARL THAT WORLDLINGS COVET.

EDWARD J. LODER.

1. The pearl that worldlings cov - et Is not the pearl for me,— Its beau - ty fades as quick - ly As sunshine on the sea; But there's a pearl sought by the wise, 'Tis called the pearl of greatest price, Tho' few its val - ue see, Oh! that's the pearl for me, Oh! that's the pearl for me, Oh! that's the pearl for me.

2. The crown that decks the mon - arch Is not the crown for me, It daz - zles but a mo - ment, Its brightness soon will flee. But there's a crown prepared a - bove For all who walk in hum - ble love, For - ev - er bright 't will be, Oh! that's the crown for me, Oh! that's the crown for me, Oh! that's the crown for me.

3. The road that ma - ny trav - el Is not the road for me, It leads to death and sor - row, In it I would not be. But there's a road that leads to God, 'Tis mark'd by Christ's most precious blood, The pas - sage here is free, Oh! that's the road for me, Oh! that's the road for me, Oh! that's the road for me.

4. The hope that sin - ners cher - ish Is not the hope for me, Most sure - ly will they per - ish, Un - less from sin made free. But there's a hope which rests in God, And leads the soul to keep his word, And sin - ful pleasures flee, Oh! that's the hope for me, Oh! that's the hope for me, Oh! that's the hope for me.

spoken in the early ages of the world but that music was adopted as its vehicle, showing thereby the universal consciousness that in that way the straightest and most effectual road would be found to the heart and affections of man." Even the rugged heart of Carlyle opened to the divine influence of music, when he wrote, "Music is well said to be the speech of angels;" and again, "See deep enough and you see musically; the heart of Nature being everywhere music, if you can only reach it." George Eliot spoke truly that, "There is no feeling, perhaps, except the extremes of fear and grief, that does not find relief in music—that does not make a man sing or play the better." J. G. Holland saw that music is "a thing of the soul—a rose-lipped shell that murmurs of the eternal sea—a strange bird singing the songs of another shore;" and all the poets from Chaucer to the lamented Longfellow, recognize the fact that "music is the universal language of mankind."

IN THE SCHOOLS.—No one thing has done more for music in the past twenty years than its introduction as an integral part of our common school education. In the large cities and suburban towns little seems left to desire in that direction. From the time children at the age of five enter the primary school till at the age of sixteen or eighteen they graduate from the high or normal school, music is as much a part of their training as the multiplication table and spelling book. The next generation will see what we foresee, and reap the harvest this generation is so wisely sowing. If, as we contend, music is in itself purifying and elevating, if it can displace and crowd out baser pleasures by giving innocent recreation and excitement to a people that must be amused, a people who must be busy for good or for evil, we can not have too much of it. It can not enter too largely or too deeply into the system of common-school education. In curious juxtaposition in an English paper a short time since was a statement that Dean Stanley had no appreciation of music, and was averse to its introduction into state systems of education; in another column was a report of one of Dean Stanley's addresses on the condi-

STEAL AWAY.

Slave Hymn.

Steal a - way, steal a - way, steal a - way to Je - sus!

Steal a - way, steal a - way home, I've not got long to stay here.

1. My Lord calls me, He calls me by the thun - der; The
2. Green trees are bend - ing, Poor sin - ners stand trem - bling; The
3. My Lord calls me, He calls me by the light - ning; The

trum - pet sounds it in my soul: I've not got long to stay here.

tion of the working classes, lamenting with an evident surprise that while so much had been done within the last twenty years to lessen intemperance among the gentry, so little comparatively had been effected among the laboring class. The inference is natural and not far-fetched which assumes a need among that very working class which had remained unheeded, unsupplied. The gentleman has his elegant home, his intellectual entertainments; an atmosphere of grace and beauty surrounds him, or is easily attainable; his craving for excitement, for a life apart from his labor, is gratified with scarcely an effort on his part. The man less fortunately situated needs recreation and stimulus even more than the other. Warmth, light, companionship, he must have. The gin-palace offers them, ruining body and soul, while it affects to comfort both. Tear down the rum-shop, turn the trades-union into a choral society, bring good music with attractive surroundings before him, educate his children to take part in grand old folk-songs, glees, and madrigals, and in a generation a strange revolution would be wrought.—*Ellis Gray.*

GLORY GILDS THE SACRED PAGE.

"Manoah."
Wm. Cowper, 1779.

1. A glo - ry gilds the sa - cred page, Ma - jes - tic like the sun;
2. The hand that gave it still sup - plies The gra - cious light and heat;
3. Let ev - er - last - ing thanks be Thine, For such a bright dis - play,
4. My soul re - joi - ces to pur - sue The steps of Him I love,

It gives a light to ev' - ry age; It gives, but bor - rows none.
Its truths up - on the na - tions rise— They rise, but nev - er set.
As makes a world of dark - ness shine With beams of heav - enly day.
Till glo - ry breaks up - on my view, In bright - er worlds a - bove.

HASTEN, SINNER, TO BE WISE.

Ignatius Pleyel.
Thomas Scott, 1776.

1. Has - ten, sin - ner, to be wise; Stay not for the mor - row's sun:
2. Has - ten mer - cy to im - plore; Stay not for the mor - row's sun;
3. Has - ten, sin - ner, to re - turn; Stay not for the mor - row's sun;
4. Has - ten, sin - ner, to be blest: Stay not for the mor - row's sun;

Wis - dom, if you still des - pise, Har - der is it to be won.
Lest thy sea - son should be o'er, Ere this even - ing's stage be run.
Lest thy lamp should cease to burn, Ere sal - va - tion's work is done.
Lest per - di - tion thee ar - rest, Ere the mor - row is be - gun.

VESPER BELL.

1. Hark! the peal - ing, Soft - ly steal - ing, Evening bell, Sweetly ech - oed down the dell.
2. Wel - come, welcome Is thy mu - sic, Sil - v'ry bell! Sweetly tell - ing day's fare - well.
3. Day is sleep - ing, Flow'rs are weeping Tears of dew; Stars are peeping ev - er true.
4. Grove and mountain, Field and fonntain, Faint - ly gleam In the rud - dy sun - set beam.

FRANZ SCHUBERT, the great lyrist, was born at Lichtenthal, a suburb of Vienna, in 1797. His father was the schoolmaster of his native village, and according to Mr. Haweis, had eighteen sons and daughters. Franz was the second son, and shared the family passion for music. When he was five years old, his father prepared him for elementary instruction, and at six he was sent to school, where he was always one of the first amongst his fellow students. The old schoolmaster was his son's first instructor in music, as in everything else, the teacher finding that the pupil "had somehow mastered the rudiments for himself." The choir-master, who was Schubert's next teacher, observed that "whenever he wanted to teach him anything, he knew it already;" and Salieri, to whom he owed most information, admitted that the boy "was a born genius, and could do whatever he chose." Mr. Haweis, who supplies these particulars in his book, "Music and Morals," argues from this early and extraordinary musical development, similar to that of Mozart and Mendelssohn, that "nature seemed to feel that a career so soon to be closed by untimely death must be begun with the tottering steps and the early lisp of childhood." But, no doubt, the precocity, with its premature undisciplined independence, had its serious disadvantages;

COME AND SEE ME.

CHILDHOOD SONGS.

1. Come and see me, Ma-ry Ann, this af-ter-noon at three, Come as ear-ly as you can, and
2. Bring with you your sis-ter Jane, my gar-den she must see, And hear the mer-ry birds a-gain, up-

stay till af-ter tea, We'll jump the rope, we'll dress the doll, we'll feed my sis-ter's birds, And
on the ap-ple tree. We'll hunt the meadow, cross the brook, we'll seek the woods a-far, Where

read my lit-tle sto-ry book, so full of ea-sy words, So come and see me, Ma-ry Ann, this
in a sun-ny lit-tle nook, the blue-eyed violets are. So come and see me, Ma-ry Ann, this

af-ter-noon at three, Come as ear-ly as you can, and stay till af-ter tea.

and it is well known that Schubert before he died deeply regretted, and was taking earnest steps to remedy, his defective knowledge of counterpoint and of the higher branches of the study of music. His superficial practical acquaintance with music was made so speedily that, at the age of eleven, he was not only a good singer in the choir of the imperial chapel, but played well on the piano and other musical instruments; and before he was fifteen he was so unexceptionable a violinist, that he would take the part of "first violin" in the orchestral practicings. In 1816, Schubert, then nineteen years of age, wrote what was to prove one of his greatest successes, but which like his other successes, received only a gradual acknowledgment. Mr. Haweis has this interesting account of the composition of the now famous air of the "Erl King:" One afternoon, Schubert was alone in the little room alloted to him in his father's house, and happening to take up a volume of Goethe's poems, he read the "Erl King." The rushing sound of the wind, and the terrors of the enchanted forest, were instantly changed for him into realities. Every line of the poem seemed to flow into strange unearthly music as he read, and, seizing a pen, he dashed down the song nearly as it is now sung, in just the time that was necessary for the mechanical writing of the music.

PULL AWAY, BRAVE BOYS.

Rossini.
"William Tell."

Animato.

1. Pull a - way, pull a - way, pull a - way, brave boys, Pull a - way, pull a - way, our hearts are
2. Pull a - way, pull a - way, pull a - way, brave boys, Pull a - way, pull a - way, to the bending

gay; Pull a - way, pull a - way thro' the dash - ing spray, On this glo - rious sum - mer day.
oar; Pull a - way, pull a - way, let us heed no more, The mu - sic from the shore.

Pull a - way, pull a - way, while with joy we're singing, And our hearts beat high with glee; Pull a -
Pull a - way, pull a - way, while our pulse is danc - ing, And our hearts are light and free; Pull a -

way, pull a - way, while our songs are ring - ing, Gay - ly o'er the sound - ing sea.
way, pull a - way, thro' the wa - ters glanc - ing, Swift we go o'er the sound - ing sea.

O'er the sea, o'er the sea, re - sound - ing, re - sound - ing, re - sound - ing, O'er the

the sound - ing sea, the sea re - sound - ing,

sea, o'er the sea, re - sound - ing, re - sound - ing, re - sound - ing, Pull a -

the sound - ing sea, the sound - ing sea.

SENSE OF BEAUTY.—Beauty is an all-pervading presence. It unfolds in the numberless flowers of the spring. It waves in the branches of the trees and the green blades of grass. It haunts the depths of the earth and the sea, and gleams out in the hues of the shell and the precious stone. And not only these minute objects, but the ocean, the mountains, the cloud, the heavens, the stars, the rising and setting sun,—all overflow with beauty. The universe is its temple; and those men who are alive to it cannot lift their eyes without feeling themselves encompassed with it on every side. Now, this beauty is so precious, the enjoyments it gives are so refined and pure, so congenial with our tenderest and most noble feelings, and so akin to worship, that it is painful to think of the multitude of men as living in the midst of it, and living almost blind to it as if, instead of this fair earth and glorious sky, they were tenants of a dungeon. An infinite joy is lost to the world by the want of culture of this spiritual endowment. Suppose that I were to visit a cottage, and see its walls lined with the choicest pictures of Raphael, and every spare nook filled with statues of the most exquisite workmanship, and that I were to learn that neither man, woman, nor child ever cast an eye at these miracles of art, how should I feel their privation! how should I want to open their eyes and to help them to comprehend and feel the loveliness and grandeur which in vain courted their notice! But every husbandman is living in sight of the works of a diviner Artist; and how much would his existence be elevated could he see the glory

LITTLE BIRD ON THE GREEN TREE.

CLARIBEL

1. Lit - tle bird, lit - tle bird, on the green tree, Lis - ten, and learn it, and
2. Lit - tle bird, lit - tle bird, on the bare tree, On - ly the win - try blast
3. Chequer'd and sad may our des - ti - ny be, Sor - row and sick - ness may
4. Part - ed and si - lenced be - neath the oak tree, Nev - er those voi - ces shall

war - ble to me; What is he pleading, and what mur - murs she? Loy - al je
sigh - eth to thee, Where are the voi - ces that sang in their glee? Loy - al je
cleave un - to thee, What - e'er can daunt us whose mot - to shall be, Loy - al je
sing un - to thee, Though in each true heart the mot - to may be, "I will be

stringendo.

se - rai, du - rant ma vie, Loy - al je se - rai du - rant ma vie.
true to thee ev - er and aye, I will be true to thee ev - er and aye."

which shines forth in their forms, hues, proportions, and moral expression! I have spoken only of the beauty of Nature, but how much of this mysterious charm is found in the elegant arts, and especially in literature! The best books have most beauty. The greatest truths are wronged if not linked with beauty; and they win their way most surely and deeply into the soul when arrayed in this their natural and fit attire. Now, no man receives the true culture of a man in whom the sensibility to the beautiful is not cherished; and I know of no condition in life from which it should be excluded. Of all luxuries, this is the cheapest and most at hand; and seems to me to be the most important to those conditions where coarse labor tends to give a grossness of mind. From the diffusion of the sense of beauty in ancient Greece, and of the taste for music in modern Germany, we learn that the people at large may partake of refined gratifications which have hitherto been thought necessarily restricted to a few.—*Channing*

I HAVE always preferred cheerfulness to mirth. The latter I consider as an act, the former as a habit of the mind. Mirth is short and transient, cheerfulness fixed and permanent. Those are often raised into the greatest transports of mirth who are subject to the greatest depressions of melancholy; on the contrary, cheerfulness, though it does not give the mind such an exquisite gladness, prevents us from falling into any depths of sorrow. Mirth is like a flash of lightning that glitters for a moment; cheerfulness keeps up a kind of daylight in the mind and fills it with steady and perpetual serenity.—*Addison*

MUSIC OF THE VOICE.—I remember listening, in the midst of a crowd, many years ago, to the voice of a girl,—a mere child of sixteen summers,—till I was bewildered. She was a pure, high-hearted, impassioned creature, without the least knowledge of the world or her peculiar gift; but her own thoughts had wrought upon her like the hush of a sanctuary, and she spoke low, as if with an unconscious awe. I could never trifle in her presence. My nonsense seemed altogether out of place; and my practised assurance forsook me utterly. She is changed now. She has been admired, and has found out her beauty; and the music of her tone is gone! she will recover it by-and-by, when the delirium of the world is over, and she begins to rely once more upon her own thoughts for company; but her extravagant spirits have broken over the thrilling timidity of her childhood, and the beautiful charm is unwound.—*Willis.*

"LEAD, KINDLY LIGHT."—Dr. John H. Newman very early mastered music as a science, and attained such a proficiency on the violin that, had he not become a doctor of the church he would have been a Paganini. At the age of twelve he composed an opera. He wrote in albums, improvised masques and idyls, and only they who see no poetry in "Lead, Kindly Light" or the "Dream of Gerontius," will deny that the divine gift entered into his birthright. He wrote this famous hymn, now sung in all our churches, in 1832, when, returning from his Mediterranean trip in an orange boat, he was becalmed for some days in the straits of Bonifacio, within sight of Caprera, since known as Garibaldi's island home.

HOME'S NOT MERELY FOUR SQUARE WALLS.

CHAS. SWAIN.
AIR FROM ROSSINI.

1. Home's not mere-ly four square walls, Though with pic-tures hung and gild-ed;
2. Home's not mere-ly roof and room, Needs it some-thing to en-dear it;

Home is where af-fec-tion calls—Filled with shrines the heart hath build-ed.
Home is where the heart can bloom; Where there's some kind lip to cheer it.

Home!—go, watch the faith-ful dove, Sail-ing 'neath the heaven a-bove us;
What is home with none to meet? None to wel-come—none to greet us?

Home is where there's one to love, Home is where there's one to love us.
Home is sweet—and on-ly sweet—Where there's one we love to meet us.

Home is where there's one to love, Home is where there's one to love us.
Home is sweet—and on-ly sweet—Where there's one we love, to meet us.

11—H

SINCE the Church has been divided into many branches, each has had its sweet singers, whose music has gladdened all the rest. It was Toplady, a severe Calvinist, who gave us "Rock of Ages." Men differ about the atonement; they almost each other heretics and outcasts in their difference about it; but, when that hymn is sung, every heart rests upon the one Redeemer. It was Charles Wesley, an Arminian, who sang "Jesus, Lover of my Soul." Side by side are Watts and Wesley, Church of England and Dis-senter. F. W. Faber, a devout Catholic, wrote that hymn which breathes the highest spirit of Christian submission, "I worship Thee, sweet Will of God." Madame Guion, an unquestioning Catholic, wrote "O Lord, how full of sweet content!" Francis Xavier, one of the founders of the Jesuit order, wrote "Thou, O my Jesus! Thou didst me upon the Cross embrace." While the Church of England was con-vulsed by the greatest struggle it has known within this century, Keble, closely attached to one of the

HARK! THE HERALD ANGELS SING.

MENDELSSOHN.
CHAS. WESLEY, 1793.

1. Hark! the her-ald an-gels sing, "Glo-ry to the new-born King! Peace on earth, and
2. Christ, by highest heav'n a - dored; Christ, the ev - er - last-ing Lord; Late in time be-
3. Hail! the heav'n-born Prince of peace! Hail! the Son of Righteousness! Light and life to

mer - cy mild, God and sin - ners re - con-ciled." Joy - ful, all ye na-tions, rise,
hold him come, Offspring of the favored one. Veil'd in flesh, the Godhead see;
all he brings, Risen with healing in his wings. Mild he lays his glo - ry by,

Join the triumph of the skies; With th'angel - ic host proclaim, "Christ is born in
Hail th' incarnate De - i - ty: Pleased, as man, with men to dwell, Je - sus, our Im -
Born that man no more may die: Born to raise the sons of earth, Born to give them

Beth-le - hem."
man - u - el! } Hark! the herald an-gels sing, "Glo - ry to the new-born King!"
se - cond birth. }

contending parties, wrote the Evening Hymn which the whole Church delights to sing. A Unitarian, Sarah F. Adams, gave us "Nearer, my God, to Thee." The controversies over the orthodoxy of that hymn are as dry and cold and dead as the stones Jacob took for his pillow; and, meanwhile, souls mount up by it toward heaven as did the angels on the ladder Jacob saw as he journeyed to Padan-aram.

WE walk here, as it were, in the crypts of life: at times, from the great cathedral above us, we can hear the organ and the chanting choir; we can see the light stream through the open door, when some friend goes out before us; and shall we fear to mount the narrow staircase of the grave that leads us out of this uncertain twilight into eternal light?—*Longfellow.*

WHENEVER I think of God, I can only conceive of him as a Being infinitely great and infinitely good. This last quality of the divine nature inspires me with such confidence and with such joy that I could have written even a Miserere in *tempo allegro.*—*Haydn*

FROM GREENLAND'S ICY MOUNTAINS.

LOWELL MASON.
REGINALD HEBER, 1823.

1. From Greenland's i-cy moun-tains, From India's cor-al strand. Where Af-ric's sun-ny
2. What though the spi-cy breez-es Blow soft o'er Ceylon's isle; Though ev'-ry pros-pect
3. Shall we, whose souls are light-ed With wis-dom from on high, Shall we, to men be-
4. Waft, waft, ye winds, His sto-ry, And you, ye wa-ters, roll, Till, like a sea of

foun-tains Roll down their gold-en sand,— From ma-ny an ancient riv-er, From
pleas-es, And on-ly man is vile; In vain with lav-ish kind-ness The
night-ed, The lamp of life de-ny? Sal-va-tion, oh, sal-va-tion! The
glo-ry, It spreads from pole to pole; Till o'er our ran-somed na-ture The

ma-ny a palmy plain, They call us to de-liv-er Their land from er-ror's chain.
gifts of God are strown; The hea-then, in his blind-ness, Bows down to wood and stone.
joy-ful sound pro-claim, Till earth's re-mot-est na-tion Has learned Messi-ah's name.
Lamb for sin-ner's slain, Re-deem-er, King, Cre-a-tor, In bliss re-turns to reign.

COME, THOU ALMIGHTY KING.

"ITALIAN HYMN."
C. WESLEY, 1757. GIARDINI, 1760.

1. Come, Thou Almight-y King, Help us Thy name to sing, Help us to praise:
2. Come, Thou In-car-nate Word, Gird on Thy might-y sword; Our prayer at-tend!
3. Come, Ho-ly Com-fort-er, Thy sa-cred wit-ness bear In this glad hour!

Fa-ther all glo-ri-ous, O'er all vic-to-ri-ous, Come, and reign o-ver us, An-cient of Days!
Come, and Thy people bless, And give Thy word success; Spirit of ho-li-ness, On us de-scend!
Thou, who almight-y art, Now rule in ev-'ry heart, And ne'er from us depart, Spirit of power,

REFERRING to praise-meetings, a leading writer says: "Every new phase of religious opinion or religious life has some reason why it should exist—emphasizing some want of our being which has been, or is likely to be, neglected. And, hence, it is to be studied and intelligently turned to account. If the praise-meeting owes its existence to the fact that we have been slighting the element of praise in our religious gatherings, or to the fact that the people want to do their own singing rather than listen to the performance of a paid quartet, by all means let us learn these lessons. We think these are the facts which make Dr. Tourjée's innovation take so well with the religious people of sober New England, while the novelty of a brass band draws in the curious and helps to crowd the house. Let us then give our churches all the chances to sing they want, under the guidance of a competent and at the same time a devout leader, and in combination with such chances to speak and pray as may make the enthusiasm de-

WITH GLOWING HEART I'D PRAISE THEE.

"AUSTRIAN HYMN."
FRANCIS SCOTT KEY, 1826.

1. Lord, with glow-ing heart I'd praise thee For the bliss thy love be - stows; For the
2. Praise, my soul, the God that sought thee, Wretched wand'rer far a - stray, Found thee
3. Lord, this bo-som's ar - dent feel - ing Vain-ly would my lips ex - press, Low be -

pard'ning grace that saves me, And the peace that from it flows; Help, O God, my weak en -
lost, and kind-ly brought thee From the paths of death a - way: Praise, with love's devout-est
fore thy foot-stool kneeling, Deign thy suppliant's prayer to bless: Let thy grace, my soul's chief

deav-or, This dull soul to rap-ture raise; Thou must light the flame, or nev - er Can my
feel - ing, Him who saw thy guilt-born fear, And, the light of hope re - veal-ing, Bade the
pleasure, Love's pure flame within me raise, And, since words can nev - er meas-ure, Let my

love be warmed to praise, Thou must light the flame, or never Can my love be warmed to praise.
blood-stained Cross appear, And, the light of hope revealing, Bade the blood-stained Cross appear.
life show forth thy praise, And, since words can never measure, Let my life show forth thy praise.

veloped by a praise-meeting yield substantial results in the conversion of sinners and the strengthening of saints. There is no doubt that singing, especially the singing of a well-trained congregation, is quite as legitimate and possibly as effective a means of grace as praying or preaching. The voice of the great congregation is one of power. You can sing men into the kingdom as well as pray them in. But true Christian praise will ever contemplate religious ends. It will never degenerate into mere recreation."

"CHEERFULNESS," says Bishop Taylor, "and a festival spirit fill the soul full of harmony; it composes music for churches and hearts; it makes and publishes glorifications of God; it produces thankfulness, and serves the end of charity; and, when the oil of gladness runs over, it makes tall and bright emissions of light, and holy fires reaching up to a cloud and making joy round about. Since it is so full of holy advantage, whatsoever can innocently minister to this holy joy sets forward the work of religion."

BATTLE-HYMN OF THE REPUBLIC.

JULIA WARD HOWE.

Allegretto.

1. Mine eyes have seen the glo - ry of the com - ing of the Lord; He is
2. I have seen Him in the watch - fires of a hun - dred cir - cling camps; They have
3. I have read a fie - ry gos - pel, writ in bur - nished rows of steel; "As ye
4. He has sound-ed forth the trum - pet that shall nev - er call re - treat; He is
5. In the beau - ty of the lil - ies, Christ was born a - cross the sea, With a

tramp - ling out the vin - tage where the grapes of wrath are stored; He hath
build - ed Him an al - tar in the eve - ning dews and damps; I can
deal with my con - tem - ners, so with you my grace shall deal; Let the
sift - ing out the hearts of men be - fore his judg - ment seat; Oh, be
glo - ry in his bos - om that trans - fig - ures you and me; As He

loosed the fate - ful light-ning of His ter - ri - ble swift sword. His truth is marching on.
read His righteous sen - tence by the dim and flar - ing lamps. His day is marching on.
He - ro, born of wom - an, crush the ser - pent with his heel, Since God is marching on."
swift, my soul, to an - swer Him! be ju - bi-lant, my feet! Our God is marching on.
died to make men ho - ly, let us die to make men free, While God is marching on.

Chorus.

Glo - ry! glo - ry! Hal - le - lu - jah! Glo - ry! glo - ry! Hal - le - lu - jah!

Glo - ry! glo - ry! Hal - le - lu - jah! His truth is march - ing on.

IN an essay of Herbert Spencer's, on the origin and functions of Music, he suggests what is now perhaps generally admitted, that, as speech is the natural expression of thought, so music is the natural language of emotion. Certainly, if the words which we speak convey our ideas, the tones in which they are uttered convey our feelings in regard to them, and the various emotions of pain and pleasure, of discontent or satisfaction, of cordiality or aversion, of eager interest or utter indifference, are much more apparent in the emphasis, cadence and intonations of the voice than in the words themselves. All these may be called the music of speech, and just as words multiply in order to express the new and delicate shades of thought that increasing civilization and culture bring forth, so the intonations of voice are even more and more delicately representing the increasingly complex emotions of which we become capable. If, then, music is itself the very language of emotion, must not the habit of listening to good music, which is true to its character, have a double effect upon us, over and above the pleasure it creates—first, to develop within us and to intensify the very feelings which it is translating, and secondly, to enable us the better to convey to others the feelings which actuate us, even in the cadences and modulations of ordinary conversation? To share our *thoughts*

LITTLE BENNIE.

G. R. POULTON.

1. Once we had a fra - grant blos - som, Full of sweet - ness, full of love,
2. Tear - ful - ly we low - ly laid him, 'Neath the grass that grew so green;
3. Years have passed, and still we miss him, And our hearts ne'er throb with glee,
4. Oh, sweet Ben - nie, when we meet thee, In the joy - ous realms a - bove,

But the an - gels came and plucked it, For the beauteous realms a - bove.
And the form of gen - tle Ben - nie In our home no more was seen.
When we think of lit - tle Ben - nie, Whom on earth no more we'll see.
Glad - ly will we haste to greet thee, All our hearts a - flame with love.

Chorus.

Lit - tle Ben - nie was our dar - ling, Pride of all the hearts at home ; But the

1st time. 2d time.

breez - es, float - ing light - ly, Came and whis - pered, "Bennie, come."

with others by the use of well-chosen words, is an art which is fully recognized and cultivated; but to share our *emotions* by any truthful and adequate expression of them, is an art which the future has yet to teach us. Indeed, the very effort is regarded by many with something like contempt, and he who succeeds best in hiding his feelings is most approved. If we are swayed by anger, impatience, jealousy, envy or hatred, the less we express ourselves the better. The sternest silence at such times is the surest method of subduing the rebellious moods. But to restrain and conceal feelings of love, kindness and good-will—to preserve an impassive exterior, when the heart thrills with affection and gladness—this is to crush out sympathy, and to silence the best promptings of humanity. The language of the emotions, whatever it may be, deserves the most earnest and careful cultivation, for by means of it is developed that sympathy which is the great bond of human society. Upon it we are dependent, both for our direct happiness and our permanent well-being. This it is which leads men to deal justly and kindly with each other, which heightens every pleasure and softens every pain, which gives rise to all domestic and social happiness, and makes life's hardest passages endurable.

"KATY DARLING."

ENGLISH BALLAD.

Con espressione.

1. Oh! they tell me thou art dead, Ka-ty Dar - ling, That thy smile I may nev-er-more be-
2. I'm kneeling by thy grave, Ka-ty Dar - ling! This world is all a blank world to
3. 'Tis useless all my weeping, Ka-ty Dar - ling! But I'll pray that thy spir-it be my

hold! Did they tell thee I was false, Ka-ty Dar - ling, Or my love for thee had e'er grown
me! Oh, could'st thou hear my wailing, Ka-ty Dar - ling, Or think, love, I am sighing for
guide; And that when my life be spent, Ka-ty Dar - ling, They will lay me down to rest by thy

cold? Oh, they know not the lov-ing Of the hearts of E - rin's sons, When a
thee. Oh, me-thinks the stars are weep-ing, By their soft and lambent light; And thy
side. Oh, a huge great grief I'm bear-ing, Tho' I scarce can heave a sigh; And I'll

love like to thine, Ka-ty Dar - ling, Is the goal to the race that he runs. Oh, hear me, sweet
heart would be melting, Katy Darling, Could'st thou see thy lone Dermot this night. Oh, listen, sweet
ever be dreaming, Ka-ty Dar - ling, Of thy love ev'-ry day till I die! Farewell, then, sweet

Ka-ty, For the wild flow'rs greet me, Ka-ty Dar - ling, And the love-birds are singing on each
Ka-ty, For the wild flow'rs are sleeping, Katy Darling, And the love-birds are nest'ling in each
Ka-ty, For the wild flow'rs will blossom, Katy Darling, And the love-birds will warble on each

tree;—Wilt thou never-more hear me, Ka-ty Dar - ling? Be-hold, love, I'm waiting for thee.
tree; Wilt thou never-more hear me, Ka-ty Dar - ling, Or know, love I'm kneeling by thee!
tree; But in heav'n I shall meet thee, Ka-ty Dar - ling, For there, love, thou'rt waiting for me?

KATHLEEN MAVOURNEEN.

F. W. N. Crouch.

Andante.

1. Kath - leen Mavourneen, the grey dawn is break - ing The horn of the hun - ter is
2. Kath - leen Mavourneen, a - wake from thy slum - bers; The blue mountains glow in the

Small notes to be sung to the 2nd verse.

heard on the hill; The lark from her light wing the bright dew is shak - ing;
sun's golden light; Ah! where is the spell that once hung on my num - bers? A -

Kathleen Ma - vour - neen, what! slum - b'ring still? Kath - leen Ma -
rise in thy beau - ty, thou star of my night; A - rise in thy

con amore affette.

vourneen, what! slum - b'ring still! Or hast thou for - got - ten how
beau - ty, thou star of my night! Ma - vour - neen, Ma - vour - neen, my

soon we must sev - er? Oh! hast thou for - got - ten this day we must
sad tears are falling, To think that from E - rin and thee I must

part? It may be for years, and it may be for - ev - er; Then why art thou
part! It may be for years, and it may be for - ev - er; Then why art thou

mf *semplice.* *mf* *mf*

si - lent, thou voice of my heart? It may be for years, and it

mf *mf*

may be for - ev - er; Then why art thou si - lent, Kathleen Mavourneen?

NOW THANK WE ALL OUR GOD.

[NUN DANKET ALLE GOTT.]

MARTIN RINKART, 1644.
C. WINKWORTH, *Tr.* 1858. J. CRAGER.

1. Now thank we all our God, With heart and hands and voi - - ces.
2. O may this bounteous God, Through all our life be near us,
3. All praise and thanks to God, The Fa - ther, now be giv - - en,

Who wondrous things hath done, In whom His earth re - joi - ces:
With ev - er joy - ful hearts, And bless - ed peace to cheer us,
The Son and Him who reigns, With them in high - est Heav - en;

Who from our moth - ers' arms Hath blessed us on our way
And keep us in His grace And guide us when per - plexed,
The one e - ter - nal God, Whom earth and Heav - en adore;

With count - less gifts of love, And still is ours to - day.
And free us from all ills, In this world and the next.
For thus it was, is now, And shall be ev - er - more!

THE BEST.—As to those whose leisure, talent, or determination makes further musical progress possible or essential, the question of greatest importance that presents itself is, How and where shall each individual most judiciously expend time and money to attain the object in view? Primarily the need is the best instruction from the best masters. Poor teaching is dear at any rate. There are two distinct methods of obtaining this instruction. With a full purse and some little influence—for these musical kings are royal potentates, and must be approached discreetly and diplomatically even to insure an audience—it is a simple matter to secure instruction from a master of acknowledged ability in his special department, at a rate varying from three to five dollars for three-quarters of an hour, or even half-an-hour's instruction. This instruction is presumably of the best, and to it we owe many of our most accomplished musicians both in vocal and instrumental music, who, in their turn, serve art by imparting to others. The

THE GOLDEN SHORE.

ALFRED S. GATTY.

1. I remem-ber, I remem-ber, In years long pass'd away, A lit-tle maid and I would meet Beside the stream to play; We used to watch the sun go down Upon the gold-en tide; And count the ships that glid-ed by To reach the o-cean wide; And count the ships that glided by, To reach the o-cean wide.

2. I remem-ber, I remem-ber, A sail-or bold to be, I left the lit-tle maid behind, And crossed the dis-tant sea; But when the ship came back a-gain, And touched the gold-en shore; I found the lit-tle maid and I Would meet on earth no more; I found the lit-tle maid and I Would meet on earth no more.

3. For-ev-er, ah! for-ev-er, Those days have flown away, And now no more be-side the stream, As children shall we play; But still I know in fu-ture days, When life's dark jour-ney's o'er, That lit-tle maid and I shall meet Up-on the gold-en shore; That lit-tle maid and I shall meet Up-on that gold-en shore.

benefits of this method, like that of a private tutor, need no discussion or setting forth; the custom is time-honored, and will always, and very properly, have its advocates in general and its special fitness for individual cases. This training, however, is not possible for the masses, who, indeed, were there even a state fund to insure it, could not be accommodated with individual lessons from first-rate masters. The alternative is class instruction, the principle upon which all graded schools—indeed, all schools, public or private—are conducted. The advantages are obvious in scientific matters as well as in common branches; the lecture on chemistry or philosophy, the lesson in arithmetic or geography, is more profitable as well as more enjoyable in a class than delivered to a single individual; the evil crops out when the class is so large that only general attention can be given the pupil. All the benefits and evils accruing from class instruction in any other branch are likely to result from class training in music.—*Gray*.

EILEEN ACHORA.

J. P. KNIGHT.
Words by Mrs. CRAWFORD.

With expression, but not too slow.

1. Oh, Ei - leen A - cho - ra! at last we have part - ed, I have caught the last glance of those beau - ti - ful eyes; The ship bounds a - long, but I turn, brok - en - heart - ed, To gaze on the land where my soul's treas - ure lies. A - round me are dash-ing the wild waves of o - cean, A - round me is beam-ing the moon's ten - der light, That wak - ens the thought of im - pass-ioned e - mo - tion, Oh, Ei - leen A - cho - ra! Sweet Ei - leen, good night! Good night! good night!

2. Oh, Ei - leen A - cho - ra! hope's spell is now brok - en, I whis - per thy name to the mur - mur-ing sea; My tears dim the gems of thy last part - ing tok - en, My sighs wing their way on the night-winds to thee. The days that are past, they re - turn in my slum-bers, When roam-ing by Ban - na's sweet wa - ter of light, I woke my wild harp to their own chos - en num-bers, Oh,

BEAUTIFUL VENICE.

J. P. Knight.
J. E. Carpenter.

Moderato. *p*

1. Beau - ti - ful Ven - ice! Ci - ty of song, What
2. Beau - ti - ful Ven - ice! Queen of the earth, Where

mem' - ries of old to thy re - gions be-long, What sweet rec-ol-lec-tions
dark eyes shine brightly 'mid mu - sic and mirth, Where gay ser-en-a-ders by

cling to my heart, As thy fast - fad-ing shores from my vis - ion de-part. Oh!
light of the star, Oft min - gle their songs with the dul - cet gui-tar; All that's

po - e - sy's home is thy light col-onnades, Where the winds gently sigh as the
love - ly in life, all that's death - less in song, Fair It - a - ly's isles to thy

sweet twilight fades. I have known many homes, but the dwell - ing for me Is
reg - ions be-long. I have known many homes, but the dwell - ing for me Is

beau - ti - ful Ven - ice, the bride of the sea. Is beau - ti - ful Ven-ice, the bride of the sea! Beau - ti - ful Ven - ice, beau - ti - ful Ven - ice,

Beau - ti - ful Ven - ice, the bride of the sea! bride of the sea!

1st verse.   *2d verse.*

WHEN YOU AND I WERE YOUNG.

GREVILLE.
GEO. B. ALLEN.

Allegretto grazioso.

1. I'm stand - ing by the win - dow sill, Where oft we stood of yore— The
2. And yon - der is the old oak - tree, Be - neath whose spreading shade, When
3. I see the lit - tle moss-grown spot, Be - neath the yew-tree's shade, Where

express.

jas - mine sweet is wav - ing still Its branch - es near the door; And
our young hearts were light and free, In in - no - cence we played— And
ear - ly friends, per - chance for - got, In earth's em - brace are laid; The

near me creeps the wild - rose vine On which our wreaths were hung; Still
o - ver there the mead - ow gate, On which our play - mates swung, Still
ear - ly friends of hope and trust, Round whom our be - ing clung, All

piu lento.   *ad lib.*   *a tempo.*

round the porch its ten - drils twine, As when we both were young.
stand - ing in its rus - tic state, As when we both were young.
slum - ber in the si - lent dust, Since you and I were young.

DUTY OF PASTORS.—We do not think that congregational singing will ever prevail with power until pastors of churches appreciate its importance and universally labor to secure it. If ministers regard singing as but a decorous kind of amusement, pleasantly relieving or separating the more solemn acts of worship, it will always be degraded. The pastor, in many cases, in small rural churches may be himself the leader. In larger societies, where a musical director is employed, the pastor should still be the animating centre of the music, encouraging the people to take part in it, keeping before them their duty, and their benefit in participating in this most delightful part of public worship. It is a very general impression that the pastor is to preach and pray, but another man is to sing. Music is farmed out, and the unity of public services is marred by two systems of exercises conducted by different persons, and oftentimes without concord or sympathy with each other, and sometimes even with such contrariety that the organ and the choir effectually neutralize the pulpit. While it may not be needful that the pastor should perform the part of a musical leader, yet it is certain that there will not be a spirit of song, in the

BY THE SAD SEA WAVES.

J. BENEDICT.

Andante.

1. By the sad sea waves, I lis-ten while they moan A la-ment o'er graves of hope and pleasure gone. I was young, I was fair, I had once not a care, From the rising of the morn to the set-ting of the sun; Yet I pine like a slave By the sad sea wave, Come again, bright days of hope and pleasure gone, Come again, bright days, Come a-gain, come a-gain.

2. From my care last night by ho-ly sleep beguiled, In the fair dream-light my home upon me smil'd. Oh, how sweet 'mid the dew, Ev'ry flow'r that I knew, Breath'd a gentle welcome back to the worn and weary child. I a-wake in my grave By the sad sea wave, Come again, dear dream so peace-ful-ly that smil'd, Come again, dear dream, Come a-gain, come a-gain.

ad lib.

whole congregation, if he is himself indifferent to it, and the first step toward congregational singing must be in the direction of the ministry.—*H. W. Beecher.*

PLATO in his Republic, desires at least two harmonies—the one warlike, which will sound the word or note which a brave man utters in the hour of danger and stern resolve, or when his cause is failing and he is going to wounds or death, or is overtaken by some other evil, and at every crisis meets fortune with calmness and endurance; and another, which may be used by him in times of peace when there is no pressure of necessity, expressive of entreaty or persuasion, of prayer to God or instruction to man; which represents him when he has accomplished his aim, not carried away by success, but acting moderately and wisely, and acquiescing in the event: the strain of necessity and the strain of freedom, of the fortunate and the unfortunate, of courage and temperance; adding in another connection, "We can never become truly musical until we know the essential forms of temperance, courage, liberality, and magnificence." Surely we can to-day raise no loftier standard than this.

If the voice be not of the best, it is of small consequence. The full-voiced sound will absorb all individuality of voice. Each will be aggregated with all. The little separate waves will go to form an entire ocean of sound, a multitudinous oneness and massive whole, without any prominent individualizing. Especially is this true when the voices are under the controlling and assimilating influence of a powerful, and well-played organ; and, in congregational singing, the organ should have the largest liberty of utterance, the foundation-stops being alone employed. So then it may be taken as a fact that, in the people's music of the church, the control and use of the voice require little artistic training, but only so much musical endowment as almost everybody naturally has, and so much musical memory as to remember such simple melodies as form the staple of tunes adapted to general use. All the better, to be sure, if preliminary training has been secured, with some knowledge of the elementary rules of music. This were best done in early life, and while at school; and we hesitate not to say that it is a great mistake whenever in any school, public or private, instruction in music and singing is omitted for what is thought more practical.

ROW, ROW, CHEERLY ROW.

D. M. MULOCK.
"EMIGRANTS' SONG."

Steady Time.

1. Pull, brave boys, pull on to-geth-er, Row, row, cheer-ly row,
2. On through vir-gin for-ests go-ing, Row, row, cheer-ly row,
3. Build the hut and clear the for-est, Row, row, cheer-ly row,

Hand to hand thro' wind and weath-er, Row, row, cheer-ly row. O'er the smooth, deep
Where the might-y riv-er's flow-ing, Row, row, cheer-ly row, With the old land
Help will come when need is sor-est, Row, row, cheer-ly row, Nev-er let our

wa-ters glid-ing, Row, row, cheer-ly row, Or the ra-pids dark di-vid-ing,
far be-hind us, Row, row, cheer-ly row, Where the new-land home shall find us,
cour-age fail us, Row, row, cheer-ly row, Nev-er let one friend be-wail us,

Chorus.

Row, row, cheer-ly row. Pull, my boys, pull on to-geth-er, Row, row,

cheer-ly row, Hand to hand thro' wind and weath-er, Row, row, cheer-ly row.

THE following incident is taken from Dr. Taylor's "Elijah, the Prophet:" About two years after the close of the thirty years' war in Germany, George Neumarck lived in a poor street in Hamburg, obtaining a precarious living by playing on a violoncello. After a while he fell sick, and was unable to go his usual rounds. As this was his only means of support, he was soon reduced to great straits and was compelled to part with his instrument to a broker, who, with characteristic sharpness, lent him on it a sum much below its value for two weeks, after which, if it were not redeemed, it was to be forfeited. As he gave it up, he looked lovingly at it, and tearfully asked if he might play one more tune upon it. "You don't know," he said "how hard it is to part with it. For ten years it has been my companion; if I had nothing else I had it; and it spoke to me and sang back to me. Of all the sad hearts that have left your door there has been none so sad as mine." Then pausing a moment he seized the instrument and commenced a tune so exquisitely soft that even the pawnbroker listened in spite of himself. A few more strains, and he sang to his own melody two stanzas of his own hymn: "Life is weary, Saviour, take me." Suddenly the key changed—a few bars and the melody poured itself forth anew, and his face

O YE TEARS!

FRANZ ABT.
CHARLES MACKAY.

Andantino.

1. O ye tears! O ye tears! that have long re-fused to flow, Ye are
2. O ye tears! O ye tears! I am thank-ful that ye run; Though ye

wel-come to my heart, Thawing, thaw-ing as the snow; The ice-bound clod has
come from cold and dark, Ye shall glit-ter in the sun; The rain-bow can-not

yield-ed, And the ear-ly snow-drops spring, And the heal-ing fountains gush, And the
cheer us, If the show'rs refuse to fall, And the eyes that can-not weep, Are the

wild-er-ness shall sing; O ye tears! O ye tears! O ye tears! O ye tears!
sad-dest eyes of all; O ye tears! O ye tears! O ye tears! O ye tears!

lighted up with a smile as he sang, "Yet who knows the cross is precious." Then laying down the instrument he said, "As God will, I am still," and hurried from the shop. Going out in the darkness, he stumbled against a stranger who seemed to have been listening at the door, and who said to him, "Could you tell me where I could obtain a copy of that song? I would willingly give a florin for it." "My good friend," said Neumarck, "I will give it to you without the florin." The stranger was a valet to the Swedish ambassador, and to him the poet told the story of his trials. He in turn told his master, who being in want of a private secretary engaged Neumarck at once; and so his troubles ended. But with his first money he redeemed his instrument, and obtaining it, he called on his landlady and his friends and neighbors to hear him play on it again. Soon the room was filled, and he sang to his accompaniment his own sweet hymn,

Leave God to order all thy ways,
And hope in Him whate'er betide,
Thou'lt find Him in the evil days
Thine all sufficient strength and guide.
Who trusts in God's unchanging love
Builds on a rock that nought can move.

I LOVE THE MERRY SUNSHINE.

J. W. Lake.
Stephen Glover.

Lively.

1. I love the mer - ry, mer - ry sunshine, It   makes the heart so gay,   To hear the sweet birds
2. I love the mer - ry, mer - ry sunshine, Thro' the dewy morning's show'r, With its ro - sy smiles ad -

sing - ing On their summer hol - i - day, With their wild-wood notes of du - ty, From
vanc - ing, Like a beau - ty from her bower! It   charms the soul in   sad - ness, It

haw thorn bush and tree; Oh, the sunshine is all   beau - ty, Oh, the mer - ry, mer - ry sun for
sets the spir - it   free; Oh, the sunshine is all   gladness, Oh, the mer - ry, mer - ry sun for

me.   I love the mer - ry, mer - ry sunshine, It makes the heart so gay, To hear the sweet birds

sing - ing On their summer hol - i - day, The mer - ry, mer - ry sun, the mer - ry, mer - ry,

merry, merry sun for me, The merry, merry sun, the merry sun, The mer - ry, mer - ry sun for me.

II—I

THE SCARLET SARAFAN.

(DER ROTHE SARAFAN.)

WARLAMOFF.
RUSSIAN FOLKSONG.

"Why, my mother, wilt thou sew the scar-let sa-ra-fan? * Useless must thine
Nä - he, Mutter, nä - he nicht den ro-then Sa-ra - fan, Dei - ne Mü - he

ef-fort be, and all thy la-bor vain." "Daugh-ter, cease thy fol - ly, and
    Though thou art so mer - ry, and
ist ver - lo - ren, quälst dich nur da - ran, Töch - ter - lein, dein Köpf - chen ist
    Springst du auch so lu - stig, und

do not talk so gay, Know that life's bright morning will not al-ways stay.
seem-est thus at ease, Song will cease to cheer thee, and the dance to please.
noch nicht ganz ge - scheid, Wis - se nur, nichts e - wig währt die Ju - gend - zeit.
singst im grü - nen Wald, Tanz-lust, ach, ver - ge - het, und Ge-sang ver - hallt.

When at length the ros - es from thy cheeks do flee, Thou wilt feel its pleas-ures
Blei - chen erst die Wan-gen dir in ern-ster Zeit, Fühlst du, dass die Ju-gend

are but van - i - ty, Thou wilt feel its pleas-ures are but van-i-ty.
nichts als Ei - tel - keit, Fühlst du, dass die Ju - gend nichts als Ei - tel - keit.

Do not smile, but do be-lieve in, what thy mo-ther says; Swift-ly flies the
La - che nicht, und glau-be nur was dei - ne Mut-ter sagt, Schnell ver-geht der

* Sarafan.—The dress of the young Russian women.

bloom of youth, and beau - ty soon de - cays. Yet, my dear - est, when I view thee,
Ju - gend Spur, Dem Himmel sei's ge - klagt. Doch wenn ich dich seh' und hö - re,

I feel young a - gain; Sing and dance then, but with tri - fling cause me no more pain.
Werd' ich wie-der jung— Sing und spring, doch nimmer stö - re mir Er - in - ne - rung.

DAY OF WONDER, DAY OF GLADNESS.

B. H. HALL.

1. Day of won - der, day of glad - ness, Hail thy ev - er glo - rious light!
2. In the tri - umph of this hour, Ju - bi - lant shall swell the song,
3. Ev - 'ry peo - ple, ev - 'ry na - tion, Soon shall hear the glad - some sound;

Gone is sor - row, gone is sad - ness, End - ed is the gloom - y night!
Un - to Je - sus, hon - or, pow - er, Bless - ing, vic - to - ry be - long.
Joy - ous tid - ings of sal - va - tion, Borne to earth's re - mot - est bound.

List - en to the an - gel's sto - ry, Cast a - way all dark and dread:
Scattered are the clouds of er - ror, Sin and hell are cap - tive led:
Then shall rise, in tones ex - cell - ing, Praise for grace so free - ly shed;

Give to God the Fa - ther glo - ry! "Christ is ris - en from the dead!"
E'en the grave is free from ter - ror, "Christ is ris - en from the dead!"
And the East - er hymn be swell - ing, "Christ is ris - en from the dead!"

AN OLD SINGER.—It is in his translation of the Gospel of St. John, completed A. D. 735, that the venerable Bede appears to us as the first writer of English vernacular prose. The story of the writing of this first prose book in the English language, as related by Cuthbert, one of Bede's pupils, is full of pathetic interest: As the season of Easter was drawing near, the zealous scholar and teacher began to feel symptoms of approaching death. But he continued faithfully the performance of his daily duties, and suffered nothing to distract his attention from his accustomed labor, or to abate his usual cheerfulness and good humor. Now and then, while in the midst of his labors, with his pupils all around him, he would sing some verses of an English song—"rude rhymes that told how before the needfare, Death's stern 'must go,' none can enough bethink him what is to be his doom for good or ill. We never read without weeping," writes Cuthbert. And so the anxious days passed, and Ascension week drew near, and both master and pupils toiled with increased zeal to finish, if possible, the work in hand—the translation of St. John's Gospel. "Learn with what speed you may," said the dying man; "for I know not how long I may last. I do not want my scholars to read a lie or to work to no purpose when I am gone." The last day came, and his pupils stood around him. "There

MARCHING SONG.

From the GERMAN.

1. March on, March on, our way a-long, While gai-ly beats the drum, dum di dum!
2. March on, March on, my comrades brave, With mus-kets flash-ing bright, dum di dum!
3. March on, March on, our steps are light, Our hearts from fear are free, dum di dum!

With stead-y tramp and ring-ing song The way will short be-come, dum di dum!
The stars and stripes a-bove us wave, And flaunt the morn-ing light, dum di dum!
For free-dom's sa-cred cause we fight, For law and li-ber-ty, dum di dum!

Tra la la la la dum! Tra la la la la dum! La la la la la la la, dum di dum!

With stead-y tramp and ring-ing song The way will short be-come, dum di dum!

is still one chapter wanting," said the scribe, seeing the master's increased weakness. "It is easily done," said Bede; "take thy pen and write quickly." They wrote until eventide drew on. Then the scribe spoke again: "There is yet but one sentence to be written, dear master." "Write it quickly," was the response of the dying man. "It is finished now," at length said the youth. "Thou hast well said," faintly replied the master, "all is finished now." The sorrowing pupils supported him tenderly in their arms while he chanted the solemn "Glory to God," and with the last words of the song his breathing ceased. Such is the story of the beginning of our literature. The humble transla-

tion of the Gospel of St. John, completed under circumstances of such painful anxiety, and amid the gathering shadows of death, was the vanguard, so to speak, of that long procession of noble works which, for a thousand years, has been contributing to the development and glory of the English nation.—*Baldwin.*

MUSIC is too often looked upon as nothing but a mere passing enjoyment—something only for the moment, to be heard and perhaps little regarded—as simply a concord of sounds agreeable to the ear: but true art occupies a much higher sphere than this; and to be able to truly appreciate and enjoy it, we must know something of the laws by which it is governed.

WARREN'S ADDRESS.

JOHN PIERPONT.

Maestoso.

1. Stand! the ground's your own, my braves! Will ye give it up to slaves? Will ye look for
2. Fear ye foes who kill for hire? Will ye to your homes re - tire? Look behind you!—
3. In the God of bat - tles trust! Die we may,—and die we must: But, O where can

green - er graves? Hope ye mer - cy still? What's the mer - cy des - pots feel?
they're a - fire! And be - fore you, see Who have done it! From the vale
dust to dust Be consigned so well, As when heaven its dews shall shed

Hear it in that bat - tle-peal! Read it on yon brist-ling steel! Ask it—ye who will.
On they come! and will ye quail? Leaden rain and i - ron hail Let their welcome be!
On the martyred patriot's bed, And the rocks shall raise their head, Of his deeds to tell?

A SOLDIER'S LIFE.

M. W. BALFE.

1. A soldier's life has seen of strife, In all its forms, so much, That no gentler theme the
2. But yet the soldier's heart doth feel, When comrades round him fall; And tho' with foes he

world will deem, A sol-dier's heart can touch. In peace or war, in hall or bow'r, His
fights with steel, As friends he smiles on all. In peace or war, in hall or bow'r, His

heart is still the same, And on the wings of fame will soar, The daring sol - dier's name.
heart is still the same, And on the wings of fame will soar, The daring sol - dier's name.

MUSIC AT HOME,—Do all you can to cultivate musical taste in your children; let them hear as much music as possible. Invite some one who can play bright and easy music, and let the children hear it. The music should be attractive, melodious and animated—a few songs, some easy galops or marches, and perhaps a quiet little piece or two. Make them understand that they must listen to music in silence. They are not allowed to talk while others are speaking, and they must give the same attention when any one plays or sings. By this means they will learn to think more of music, and to appreciate it more highly. There is nothing to prevent children from taking up music as naturally as reading and writing. The notes and the alphabet should be learned at the same time. At five and six, children learn to sing naturally and easily, and little songs and exercises should be mingled with the lessons of the primary reading and spelling book. Experience teaches that nearly all children who can speak may be taught to read vocal music and to sing. Some knowledge of music should form a part of every child's education. At the same time, it is evident that it is often useless to carry a child

DOUGLAS, TENDER AND TRUE.

D. M. MULOCH.
LADY JANE SCOTT.

1. Could ye come back to me, Douglas! Douglas! In the old like - ness that I knew, I
2. Nev - er a scorn - ful word should grieve ye; I'd smile as sweet as the an - gels do,—
3. Oh, to call back the days that are not! Mine eyes were blinded, your words were few: Do you

would be so faithful, so lov - ing, Douglas! Doug-las! Douglas! ten - der and true.
Sweet as your smile on me shone ev - er, Doug-las! Douglas! ten - der and true.
know the truth now up in Heaven, Doug-las! Douglas! ten - der and true?

4. I was not half worthy of you, Douglas, Not half worthy the like of you; Now
5. Stretch out your hand to me, Douglas! Douglas! Drop forgiveness from heaven like dew, As I

all men be-side are to me like shadows, Douglas! Doug-las! ten - der and true.
lay my heart on your dead heart, Douglas! Douglas! Doug-las! ten - der and true.

through a long course of musical study when he or she has no special aptitude for it. If they do not care much for it, let them study it enough to understand at least its general principles and to store the memory with a goodly number of tunes, both of songs and of hymns, for their future pleasure and profit.

THE most popular and truly meritorious of Moore's writings were his "Irish Melodies," written from time to time between the years 1807 and 1834. Byron has said: "Moore is one of the few writers who will survive the age in which he so deservedly flourishes. He will live in the 'Irish Melodies.' They will go down to posterity with the music; both will last as long as Ireland, or as music and poetry." Alison, in his History of Europe, adds this tribute to their merit, "His Irish and National Melodies will be immortal; and they will be for this reason,—that they express the feelings which spring up in the breast of every successive generation at the most important and imaginative period of life. They have the delicacy of refined life without its fastidiousness, the warmth of natural feeling without its rudeness."

'TIS LONE ON THE WATERS.

JOHN BLOCKLEY.

Moderato.

1. 'Tis lone on the wa-ters, when eve's mournful bell Sends forth to the
2. When the wing of the sea-bird is turned to her nest, And the heart of the

sun-set a note of fare-well; When borne on the shadows and winds as they
sai-lor to all he loves best; 'Tis lone on the wa-ters, that hour hath a

sweep, There comes a fond mem-'ry of home o'er the deep, There comes a fond
spell To bring back sweet voi-ces and words of fare-well, To bring back sweet

mem'-ry of home o'er the deep; 'Tis lone on the wa-ters when
voi-ces and words of fare-well; 'Tis lone on the wa-ters when

eve's mourn-ful bell Sends forth to the sun-set a note of fare-

well, Sends forth to the sun-set a note of fare-well.

p *dolce.*

SOUND AND LIGHT.—The analogy between sound and light is perfect even in its minutest circumstance. When a certain number of vibrations of a musical chord is caused in a given time, we produce a required sound; as the vibrations of the chord vary from a quick to a slow rate we produce sounds sharp or grave. So with light; if the rate at which the ray undulates is altered, a different sensation is made upon the organ of vision. The number of aerial vibrations per second required to produce any particular note in music has been accurately calculated; and it is also known that the ear is able to detect vibrations producing sound, through a range commencing with fifteen, and reaching as far as forty-eight thousand, in a second,—the longest waves capable of producing the sensation of sound being sixty-six feet in length, and the shortest three and one-fifth inches. So also in the case of light, the frequency of vibrations of the ether required for the production of any particular color has been determined, and the length of the waves corresponding to these vibrations. The waves producing that sensation on the nerve of sight which

HAPPY DAYS GONE BY.

D. GODFREY.

Tempo di Valse.

1. O hap-py days gone by, So fond-ly dear to me;
2. I lin-ger o'er the past, Sweet vis-ions of the heart;
3. Still o'er the past 'we dwell, With fond in-creas-ing care;

con anima.

As flowers the fair-est soon-est die, So youth's bright hours no more I
I mourn o'er hours that can-not last, And yet how soon those dreams de-
To all those scenes we bid fare-well, Those death-less mem'-ries dear and

see, Fare-well, those hap-py days, How soon youth's joys de-cay;
part! Oh! will they ne'er re-turn, To glad the heart a-gain?
fair. Then let us fond-ly dream Those ear-ly vis-ions o'er;

Like mu-sic's sweet-est, ten-d'rest lays, They charm, then fade a-way.
They're cloistered deep in mem-ory's urn, In si-lence and in pain.
Like stars that burn, then hide their beam, They fade to shine no more!

we agree to call red, are the largest; orange comes next; then yellow, green, blue, indigo, violet succeed each other, the waves of each being less than the preceding. The rapidity of the vibrations is in the same order, the waves producing red light vibrating with the least, and those producing violet, at the other end of the spectrum, with the greatest rapidity. To produce red light, it is necessary that 39,000 waves be comprised within the space of a single inch, and that 460,000,000,000,000 vibrations be executed in one second of time; while for violet, 57,500 waves within an inch, and 680,000,000,000,000 vibrations per second are required. How do we reach these figures infinitely beyond human comprehension? It is known that light travels 186,000 miles per second. Each second, therefore, a length of ray amounting to 186,000 miles must enter the pupil of the eye. But in the case of red light there are 39,000 vibrations to the inch. In the space of so many miles there must be 460,000,000,000,000 of vibrations!! Rays of light of all colors, as waves of sound of every pitch, pass uniformly with the same velocity

BOUNDING BILLOWS.

MARY DERBY, 1780.

1. Bound - ing bil - lows, cease your mo - tion, Bear me not so
2. Proud has been my fa - tal pas - sion; Proud my in - jured
3. Far I go, where fate may lead me; Far a - cross the
4. Not one sigh shall tell my sto - ry, Not one tear my

swift - ly o'er; Cease thy roar - ing, foam - y O - cean, Cease thy
heart shall be; While each thought and in - cli - na - tion, While each
trou - bled deep, Where no strang - ers e'er can heed me, Where no
cheek shall stain, Si - lent grief shall be my glo - ry— Sil - ent

roar - ing, foam - y O - cean, I - will tempt thy rage no more.
thought and in - cli - na - tion, Still shall prove me wor - thy thee.
strang - ers e'er can heed me, Where no eye for me shall weep.
grief shall be my glo - ry— Grief that stoops not to com - plain.

THE BELL IS RINGING.

F. SILCHER.

1. (ROUND.)

Hark! the bell is ringing, Calling us to sing-ing, Hear the cheerful lay, Come, come, come away!

2.

Hark! the bell is ringing, Call-ing us to singing, Hear the cheerful lay, Come, come, come away!

3.

Hark! hark! the bell is ringing, Call-ing us to sing-ing, Come, come, come, come away!

1 (ROUND.) 2

Scot - land's burn - ing! Scot - land's burn - ing! Look out! look

3 4

out! Fire! fire! fire! fire! Cast on more wa - ter.

MUSIC, of all other arts, is more especially placed at the mercy of mankind. The painting, once finished, needs nothing but the light of heaven to convey it to the organ by which it is admitted to the mind. The poem, with all its holy utterances, its pathos, its passion, has its form in "words that burn." But there is no such silent independence in music. The offspring of the musician is born dumb—it reaches no ear but his own, and that a mental one—it has to appeal to others to give it voice and being. Hence it comes that the composer and his composition are separated by a medium which too often *reflects* dishonor not only upon him, but upon the art itself. He is at the mercy of the caprices of singers and players; and the material through which it gets expression, the wood, the catgut and metal—all liable to every variation of the weather—are indispensable to its very existence. The subtle form and conditions of music are remarkable. It has also, as it were, to put on mortality afresh—it is ever being born anew, but to

DAYS OF ABSENCE.

ROUSSEAU, 1775.
"ROUSSEAU'S DREAM."

1. Days of ab-sence, sad and drea-ry, Clothed in sor-row's dark ar-ray;
2. Not till that loved voice can greet me, Which so oft has charmed mine ear;
3. All my love is turned to sad-ness, Ab-sence pays the ten-der vow,

Days of ab-sence, I am wea-ry, She I love is far a-way,
Not till those sweet eyes can meet me, Tell-ing that I still am dear;
Hopes that filled the heart with glad-ness, Mem-ory turns to an-guish now;

When the heav-y sigh be ban-ished? When this bos-om cease to mourn?
Days of ab-sence then will van-ish, Joy will all my pangs re-pay;
Love may yet re-turn to greet me, Hope may take the place of pain;

Hours of bliss too quick-ly van-ished, When will aught like you re-turn?
Soon my bos-om's i-dol ban-ish Gloom, but felt when she's a-way.
An-toin-ette with kiss-es meet me, Breath-ing love and peace a-gain.

die away and leave only dead notes and dumb instruments behind. The orchestra and choristers assemble, and it is there—but gone again when they disperse. In this fugitiveness of form some have pretended to see only the frivolity of the thing; but how deep, on the contrary, must be the foundations of that pleasure which has so precious a form of outward expression;—how intensely must that enjoyment be interwoven with the godlike elements of our being, in which mere outward sense has so fleeting a share! The very limitation of its natural resources is the greatest proof of its spiritual power. Were it not for the grossness of our natures, we should take it in, not by the ear only, but by every pore of our frames. And yet our intensest sympathies are awakened, and this mysterious influence is exerted merely through a slight and evanescent vibration of the air! "Whence art thou! thou divine, mysterious thing?" is a question we must ever ask in vain, because its paths are lost in the depths of our being. We only know, and can know, of music that its science is an instinct of our nature—its subjects the emotions of our hearts.—*Wysham.*

THERE is no power of love so hard to get and keep as a kind voice. A kind hand is deaf and dumb. It may be rough in flesh and blood, yet do the work of a soft heart, and do it with a soft touch. But there is no one thing that love so much needs as a sweet voice to tell what it means and feels; and it is hard to get and keep it in the right tone. One must start in youth and be on the watch night and day, at work and play, to get and keep a voice that shall speak at all times the thoughts of a kind heart. But this is the time when a sharp voice is most apt to be got. You often hear boys and girls say words at play with a quick, sharp tone, as if it were the snap of a whip. When one of them gets vexed you will hear a voice that sounds as if it were made up of a snarl and whine, and a bark. Such a voice often speaks worse than the heart feels. It shows more ill-will in the tone than in the words. It is in mirth also that one gets a voice or tone that is sharp, which sticks to him through life, and stirs up ill-will and grief, and falls like a drop of gall on

THE GIRL I LEFT BEHIND ME.

"BRIGHTON CAMP," 1760?

Allegretto.

1. I'm lone - some since I cross'd the hill, And o'er the moor and val - ley; Such heav - y thoughts my heart do fill, Since part - ing with my Sal - ly. I seek no more the fine and gay, For each does but re - mind me How swift the hours did pass a - way, With the girl I've left be - hind me.

2. Oh! ne'er shall I for - get the night, The stars were bright a - bove me, And gent - ly lent their silv - 'ry light, When first she vowed she loved me. But now I'm bound to Brigh - ton camp, Kind Heaven, may fa - vor find me, And send me safe - ly back a - gain To the girl I've left be - hind me.

3. The bee shall hon - ey taste no more, The dove be - come a ran - ger, The dash - ing waves shall cease to roar, Ere she's to me a stran - ger; The vows we've reg - is - ter'd a - bove Shall ev - er cheer and bind me, In con - stan - cy to her I love, The girl I've left be - hind me.

4. My mind her form shall still re - tain, In sleep - ing or in wak - ing, Un - til I see my love a - gain, For whom my heart is break - ing. If ev - er I should see the day, When Mars shall have re - signed me, For ev - ermore I'll glad - ly stay With the girl I've left be - hind me.

the sweet joys at home. Such as these get a sharp home voice for use, and keep their best voices for those they meet elsewhere, just as they would save their best pies and cakes for guests, and all their sour food for their own board. Use your guests' voice at home. Watch it, day by day, as a pearl of great price, for it will be worth more to you in days to come than would the best pearl hid in the sea. A kind voice is a joy like a lark's song to a hearth and home. It is to the heart what light is to the eye. Sweeter than song—it is a light that sings as well as shines. Train it to sweet tones early and it will keep in tune thro' life.

"THE girl I left behind me," is thought to be of Irish origin. It was written when there were camps along the coast of England, and was long known as "Brighton Camp." For upwards of a century it has been a favorite with military bands and is usually played on such special occasions as the departure of troops from home or from camp, as well as upon the sailing of a transport as she weighs her anchor.

CHILD OF EARTH WITH THE GOLDEN HAIR.

Chas. E. Horn.

Allegro con anima.

1. Child of earth with the gold - en hair, Thy soul's too pure and thy
2. I'll rob of its sweets the hon - ey bee, I'll crush the wine from the

face too fair, To dwell with the crea - tures of mor - tal mould, Whose
cow - slip tree, I'll pull thee ber - ries, I'll heap thy bed Of

lips are warm as their hearts are cold. Roam, roam to our fai - ry home.
down - y moss and the pop - pies red. Roam, roam to our fai - ry home.

Child of earth with the gold - en hair, Thou shalt dance with the fai - ry queen Thro'
Child of earth with the gold - en hair, Dim sleep shall woo thee, dar - ling boy, In her

sum - mer nights on the moon - lit green, To mu - sic mur - mur-ing sweet - er
mild - est mood, with dreams of joy, And when with the morn - ing ends her

far Than ev - er was heard 'neath the morn - ing star.
reign, Pleas - ure shall bid thee wel - - come a - gain.

Animato.

Roam, roam to our fai - ry home, Child of earth with the gold - en hair,

Roam, roam to our fai - ry home, Child of earth with the gold - en hair.

MERRILY EVERY BOSOM BOUNDETH.

GERMAN AIR.

1. Mer - ri - ly ev - 'ry bo - som bound-eth, Mer - ri - ly, oh! mer - ri - ly, oh!
2. Wea - ri - ly ev - 'ry bo - som sigh - eth,* Wea - ri - ly, oh! wea - ri - ly, oh!
3. Cheer-i - ly, then, from hill and val - ley, Cheer-i -ly, oh! cheer-i - ly, oh!

Where the song of Free-dom sound-eth, Mer - ri - ly, oh! mer - ri - ly, oh!
When the dove of Peace, it fli - eth, Wea - ri - ly, oh! wea - ri - ly, oh!
As when lake and zephyr dal - ly, Cheer-i - ly, oh! cheer-i - ly, oh!

There the gathering smiles of Peace are beaming, Where the star - ry flag is gai - ly streaming,
There no cheerful songs of Free-dom greeting, Childhood's happy smile how quickly fleet-ing,
While the children shout in gladsome manner Where they wave the nation's star-ry ban-ner,

Ev - e - ry joy the land re-sonnd - eth, Mer - ri - ly, oh! mer - ri - ly, oh!
Ev - e - ry flow - er of life then dieth, Wea - ri - ly, oh! wea - ri - ly, oh!
Round the flag of Free-dom ral - ly, Cheer-i - ly, oh! cheer-i - ly, oh!

*The minor is used in this verse with effect, where there is an instrument to guide, by substituting E flat for E.

LUTHER found very much delight in music. After his marriage it was his custom once a week to have a musical entertainment at his house, when instrumental and vocal selections were given, and Christmas was always kept with great gayety. Luther himself was an excellent singer, accompanying himself upon the guitar, and he composed music for several of his hymns. The most celebrated of these compositions is his Battle Hymn. No translator has ever been able to reproduce in forcible English the spirit and sublimity of the original. The Marseillaise of the Reformation, as Heine well says, was this veritable war song, *Ein Feste Burg.* "Upon its theme," remarks Dr. Leonard W. Bacon, "the composers of the sixteenth and seventeenth centuries practiced their artifice. The supreme genius of Sebastian Bach made it the subject of study. And in our own times it has been used with conspicuous effect in Mendelssohn's Reformation Symphony, in an overture by Raff, in the noble Festouverture of Nicolai, and in Wagner's Kaiser Marsch; and it is introduced with recurring emphasis in Meyerbeer's masterpiece of the 'Huguenots.'" The earliest hymn-book of the Reformation—if not the earliest of all printed hymn-books—was published at Wittenberg in 1524, and contained eight hymns, four of them from the pen of Luther himself. An interesting letter from the composer, John Walter, capellmeister to the Elector of Saxony, embodies his reminiscenses of his illustrious friend as a church musician. When Walter asked Luther how he came by his good taste and knowledge to fit all the notes to the text according to the "just accent and concent,' the answer was: "I learned this of the poet Virgil, who has the power so artfully to adapt his verses and his words to the story that he is telling."

A MIGHTY FORTRESS IS OUR GOD.

"EIN FESTE BURG."
MARTIN LUTHER, 1529

1. A migh-ty Fort-ress is our God, A trus-ty Shield and Weap-on;
2. With might of ours can naught be done, Soon were our loss ef-fect-ed;
3. Tho' dev-ils all the world should fill, All watching to de-vour us,
4. The Word they still shall let re-main, And nev-er thanks have for it,

He helps us free from ev-'ry need That hath us now o'er-tak-en.
But for us fights the Val-iant One Whom God Him-self e-lect-ed.
We trem-ble not, we fear no ill, They can-not over-pow-er us.
He's by our side up-on the plain, With His good gifts and spir-it.

The old bit-ter foe Means us dead-ly woe: Deep guile and great
Ask ye, Who is this? Je-sus Christ it is The Lord Sa-ba-
This world's prince may still Scowl fierce as he will, He can harm us
Take they then our life, Goods, fame, child and wife; When their worst is

might Are his dread arms in fight, On earth is not his e-qual.
oth, And there's none oth-er God, He holds the field for ev-er.
none, He's judged, the deed is done, One lit-tle word o'er-throws him.
done, They yet have noth-ing won, The King-dom ours re-main-eth.

ROCK OF AGES.

A. M. TOPLADY, 1776.
THOMAS HASTINGS, 1830.

1. Rock of A - ges, cleft for me, Let me hide my - self in Thee;
2. Not the la - bors of my hands Can ful - fil Thy law's de - mands;
3. Noth - ing in my hand I bring, Sim - ply to Thy cross I cling;
4. While I draw this fleet - ing breath, When mine eye - lids close in death;

Let the wa - ter and the blood, From Thy wound - ed side which flowed,
Could my zeal no res - pite know, Could my tears for - ev - er flow,
Nak - ed come to Thee for dress, Help - less, look to thee for grace:
When I rise to worlds un - known, See Thee on Thy judgment throne,

Be of sin the dou - ble cure, Save from wrath and make me pure.
All for sin could not a - tone, Thou must save, and Thou a - lone.
Foul, I to the foun - tain fly; Wash me, Sa - viour, or I die.
Rock of A - ges, cleft for me, Let me hide my - self in Thee.

HOLY BIBLE, BOOK DIVINE.

J. F. BARTON.

1. Ho - ly Bi - ble, book di - vine; Pre - cious treas - ure, thou art mine;
2. Mine, to chide me when I rove; Mine, to show a Sa - viour's love;
3. Mine, to com - fort in dis - tress, If the Ho - ly Spir - it bless;
4. Mine, to tell of joys to come, And the reb - el sin - ner's doom;

Mine, to tell me whence I came; Mine, to teach me what I am.
Mine art thou to guide my feet, Mine, to judge, con - demn, ac - quit.
Mine, to show by liv - ing faith Man can tri - umph o - ver death.
Ho - ly Bi - ble, book di - vine, Pre - cious treas - ure, thou art mine.

Music is a language, the ideal of speech: we can imagine its existence before articulate speech was known. Birds sang in the garden of Eden before Adam gave them a name. A singing-bird was the first music-master; the wind breathing through water-reeds, sighing through the forest, hissing through tall grasses, the rhythmic beat of the crested waves, the monotonous bass of the water-fall, made harmony and melody before Pythagoras dreamed of the music of the spheres, or Hermes declared music to be the knowledge of the order of all things. We call it a pretty conceit of the old philosopher who believed the order of the stars to be a written scroll of music, two stars (which are said to have appeared centuries after his death in the places he designated) only wanting to complete the celestial harmony. There is an extremely poetic belief among the Highlanders that the sense of hearing becomes so exquisitely keen at the approach of death that nature's divine symphony can be heard with all its ravishing sweetness,

·BLUE-EYED MARY.

GERMAN AIR.

1. "Come, tell me, blue-eyed stranger, Say, whither dost thou roam? O'er this wide world a ranger, Hast thou no friends, no home?" "They called me blue-eyed Mary, When friends and Fortune smiled; But, ah! how fortunes vary— I now am Sorrow's child."

2. "Come here, I'll buy thy flowers, And ease thy hapless lot; Still wet with vernal showers, I'll buy forget-me-not." { "Kind sir, then take these posies,—They're fading, like my youth; But never, like these roses, Shall wither Mary's truth." } { Born thus to weep my fortune, Though poor, I'll virtuous prove; I early learn'd this cau-tion, That pity is not love." }

3. "Look up, thou poor forsaken, I'll give thee house and home, And if I'm not mistaken, Thou'lt never wish to roam." "Once more I'm happy Mary, Once more has Fortune smiled; Who ne'er from virtue vary, May yet be Fortune's child."

dulling the sense of pain and reconciling the soul to its departure. From this superstition, if we will, comes their custom, as the last moment approaches, of bearing the dying from the close shealing to the open air, where undisturbed he can listen, in the words of Humboldt, to "the thousand voices of nature speaking to the thoughtful and pious soul of man."

THE following is from "Paul Faber, Surgeon," by George Macdonald: The best of her undoubtedly appeared in her music, in which she was fundamentally far superior to Helen, though by no means so well trained, taught, or practiced in it; whence Helen had the unspeakable delight, one which only a humble, large and lofty mind can ever have, of consciously ministering to the growth of another in the very thing wherein that other is naturally the superior. The way to the blessedness that is in music, as to all other blessedness, lies through weary labors, and the master must suffer with the disciple. Helen took Juliet like a child, set her to scales and exercises, and made her practice hours a day.

LOVE NOT.

JOHN BLOCKLEY,
CAROLINE NORTON.

Andantino.

1. Love not! love not! Ye hap less sons of clay, Hope's gayest wreaths are made of earthly
2. Love not! love not! the thing you love may die, May per-ish from the gay and gladsome
3. Love not! love not! the thing you love may change, The ro - sy lip may cease to smile on
4. Love not! love not! oh, warn-ing vain-ly said In present hours, as in years gone

flow'rs; Things that are made to fade and fade a - way, Ere they have blossom'd for a
earth, The si - lent stars, the blue and smiling sky, Beams on its grave, as once up -
you, The kind - ly beaming eye grow cold and strange, The heart still warmly beat yet
by: Love flings a ha - lo round the dear one's head, Fault - less, im - mor-tal till they

few short hours, Ere they have blossom'd for a few short hours. Love not! love not!
on its birth, Beams on its grave, as once up - on its birth. Love not! love not!
not be true, The heart still warmly beat, yet not be true. Love not! love not!
change or die, Faultless, im - mortal till they change or die. Love not! love not!

WHEN THE GREEN LEAVES.

1. When the green leaves come again, my love, When the green leaves come again, Why put on a dark and
2. Ah! the spring will still be like the last, Of its prom - ise false and vain, And the summer die in
3. So the seasons pass, and so our lives, Yet I nev - er will complain; But I sigh, while yet I

cloud - y face, When the green leaves, When the green leaves, When the green leaves come again?
win - ter's arms, Ere the green leaves, Ere the green leaves, Ere the green leaves come a - gain.
know not why, When the green leaves, When the green leaves, When the green leaves come again.

Nay, lift up your thankful eyes, my love!
Thinking less of grief or pain;
For as long as hill and vale shall last,
Will the green leaves come again.

Sure as earth lives under winter's snow,
Sure as love lives under pain,—
It is good to sing with every thing,
When the green leaves come again.

II—K

ANOTHER grand voice of nature is the thunder. Ignorant people often have a vague idea that thunder is produced by the clouds knocking together, which is very absurd, if you remember that clouds are but water-dust. The most probable explanation of thunder is much more beautiful than this. Heat forces the air-atoms apart. Now, when a flash of lightning crosses the sky, it suddenly expands the air all round it as it passes, so that globe after globe of sound-waves is formed at every point across which the lightning travels. Light travels so rapidly (192,000 miles in a second) that a flash of lightning is seen by us and is over in a second, even when it is two or three miles long. But sound comes slowly, taking five seconds to travel a mile, and so all the sound-waves at each point of the two or three miles fall on our ear one after the other, and make the rolling thunder. Sometimes the roll is made even longer by the echo, as the sound-waves are reflected to and fro by the clouds on their way; and in the mountains we know how the peals echo and re-echo until they die away.

THE NINETY AND NINE.

IRA D. SANKEY.
ELIZABETH C. CLEPHANE, 1868.

1. There were ninety and nine that safe - ly lay In the shel - ter of the fold, But one was out on the hills a - way,. Far off from the gates of gold— A - way on the mountains wild and bare, A - way from the ten - der Shepherd's care, A - way from the ten - der Shepherd's care.

2. "Lord, Thou hast here Thy nine - ty and nine; Are they not e - nough for Thee?" But the Shepherd made an - swer: "'Tis of Mine Has wan - dered away from Me; And although the road be rough and steep, I go to the desert to find My sheep, I go to the desert to find My sheep."

3. But none of the ran - somed ev - er knew How deep were the wa - ters cross'd; Nor how dark was the night that the Lord pass'd thro',. Ere He found His sheep that was lost; Out in the des - ert He heard its cry—'Twas help - less and sick, and ready to die, 'Twas helpless and sick, and ready to die.

4. But all thro' the mountains, thunder - riv - en, And up from the rock - y steep, There rose a cry to the Gate of Heaven, "Re - joice! I have found My sheep!" And the an - gels echoed a - round the throne, "Re - joice, for the Lord brings back His own! Rejoice, for the Lord brings back His own!"

"WE have selected music," says Rev. Henry Ward Beecher, in his preface to the Plymouth Collection, "with reference to the wants of families, of social meetings, and of the lecture-room, as well as of the great congregation. But the tunes are chiefly for congregational singing. We have gathered up whatever we could find of merit, in old or new music, that seemed fitted for this end. Not the least excellent are the popular revival melodies, which, though they have been often excluded from classic collections of music, have never been driven out from among the people. These have been gathered up, and fitly arranged, having already performed most excellent service. They are now set forth with the best of all testimonials—the affection and admiration of thousands who have experienced their inspiration. Because they are home-bred and popular, rather than foreign and stately, we like them none the less. And we cannot doubt that many of them will carry up to heaven the devout fervor of God's people until the millennial day."

Music is one of the best of arts. The notes make the words living. Music drives away the spirit of sadness, as we see by King Saul. Music is the best recreation for sad men; thereby, the heart becomes contented, refreshed, and restored. Music makes a man more tender and sweet-natured, more moral and reasonable. I love music at all times. A man who knows this art is qualified for all good things. It is necessary to keep music in schools. I do not look at a school-teacher who can not sing. I would not part with my little music for great riches. Singing is the best art and training. Dear, sing me a song as David did when playing his harp. Music is a gift and a donation of the Lord, and not from men. It drives away the devil, and makes people merry; they forget anger, impurity, pride and other vices. And we see how David and all other saints have put their pious thoughts into poems and songs. — *Martin Luther, Dec.* 18, 1538.

WAKE, FOR THE NIGHT IS FLYING.

"WACHET AUF."
PHILIP NICOLAI, 1599.

1. Wake, a wake, for night is fly - ing, The watch - men on the heights are cry - ing; A - wake, Je - ru - sa - lem, at last! Mid - night hears the welcome voi - ces, And at the thrilling cry re - joi - ces; Come forth, ye virgins, night is past! The Bridegroom comes, a-wake, Your lamps with gladness take; Hal - le - lu - jah! And for His marriage feast pre - pare, For ye must go to meet Him there.

2. Zi - on hears the watch - men sing - ing, And all her heart with joy is spring - ing; She wakes, she ris - es from her gloom; For her Lord comes down all glo - rious, The strong in grace, in truth vic - to - rious; Her Star is ris'n, her Light is come! Ah, come, Thou bless - ed Lord, O Je - sus, Son of God, Hal - le - lu - jah! We fol - low till the halls we see Where Thou hast bid us sup with Thee.

3. Now let all the heavens a - dore Thee, And men and an - gels sing be - fore Thee, With harp and cymbal's clear - est tone; Of one pearl each shin - ing por - tal, Where we are with the choir im - mor - tal Of an - gels round Thy dazzling throne; Nor eye hath seen, nor ear Hath yet attained to hear What there is ours, But we re - joice and sing to Thee, One hymn of joy e - ter - nal - ly.

PROGRESS.—Granting the need of more general musical culture, if we as a nation would not only become capable of appreciating the highest expression of art, but would cherish the hope of one day giving birth to the true artist, child of his times and his people, how shall we best secure that training and that broad general culture characteristic of the universal art above all others? In primary and grammar schools this is begun; in the high and normal schools in the large cities this training progresses as far and as rapidly as could be reasonably expected. It embraces to a limited extent the theory of music, the rudiments of harmony, and more or less proficiency in sight singing and training as chorus or part singers, rarely as soloists. With instrumental music no acquaintance is attempted as yet, but the fields are ready for sowing. Under judicious leadership, such as our large cities are able to command, thousands of boys and girls are familiarized with good music, and have taken part in the grand choruses which "sing straight up to heaven." Mendelssohn, Mozart, Handel, and Haydn have become as household words. The best of the light modern music, adapted for their

JOY WAIT ON THY MORROW.

FRENCH AIR.

1. Joy wait on thy morrow! when morning shall beam, And smile thro' its tears on the earth,
2. Joy wait on thy morrow! when noon-tide shall glow, And shadows grow fainter and few.
3. Joy wait on thy morrow! when evening shall sigh, And mantle the slumber-ing world.

May pleasure like sunshine, may hap-pi-ness gleam, And scat-ter the gloom from thy hearth.
May Love's glad'ning presence rest over thee, so That Grief find no place for its hue;
May Sym-pa-thy fold thee, and, faith-ful-ly nigh, Watch o'er thee, night's banner unfurled;

The love-missioned spir-its, that give to the flowers A beauty, and brightness the darkness denied,
May Friendship, still faithful, strew flowers in thy way, With wishes of hope, and of faith, and of truth;
While dreams of the future make light round thy soul, An element kindred, and cheering, and kind.

Re-store to thy bos-om the hopes which in hours Of sor-row, have withered and died.
We know that thy fu-ture is mirrored to-day If thy heart keep the freshness of youth.
Where mu-sic shall linger, and, as the years roll, Sweet peace, and contentment of mind.

use, is given for their profit and enjoyment, making possible such programmes as those afforded by our annual school festivals, when twelve or fifteen hundred fresh, pure voices make such music as we dream of when we think of "the voice of harpers harping with their harps, and they sung as it were a new song before the throne." With many, because of other interests and occupations, special musical instruction ends here, but not the far-reaching result. The glees and four-part songs, so skillfully and thoroughly learned at school, are as sweet within the walls of the humblest home, in the woodland ramble, when the rare holiday comes, or in the workshop. The purest and simplest form of musical enjoyment is thus made possible, with all harmonious requirements, where even four are found with one heart and mind, with music in their souls, though not a single musical instrument should offer its sustaining accompaniment. When the genius of music crowns the gospel of work, there will be fewer strikes; grimy faces will be less haggard; under the unconscious influence of beauty, harmony, and rhythm, labor will be more cheerfully, more faithfully performed—Gray.

MAKE THE BEST OF IT.

C. J. DUNPHY.

1. Life is but a fleet - ing dream, Care destroys the zest of it; Swift it gli - deth
2. If your friend has e'er a heart, There is something fine in him; Cast a - way his
3. Hap - pi - ness des - pis - es state, Tho' 'tis no dis - par - agement When the man that's
4. Trust - ing in the Power a - bove, Which, sustaining all of us, In one common

like a stream—Mind you make the best of it Talk not of ' your wea - ry woes,
dark - er part, Cling to what's di - vine in him: Friendship is our best re - lief,
wise and great Has both joy and mer - ri - ment. Rank is not the spell re-fined,
bond of love Bin - deth great and small of us, Then, what-ev - er may be - fall,

Troubles, or the rest of it, If we have but brief re - pose, Let us make the best of it.
Make no heartless jest of it, It will brighten ev - 'ry grief If we make the best of it.
Mon - ey's not the test of it, But a calm, cou - tent - ed mind That will make the best of it.
Sor - rows, or the rest of it, We shall o - vercome them all, If we maké the best of it.

HAIL TO THE BRIGHTNESS.

THOS, HASTINGS.

1. Hail to the brightness of Zi-on's glad morning! Joy to the lands that in darkness have lain;
2. Hail to the brightness of Zi-on's glad morning! Long by the proph-ets of Is-rael fore - told;
3. Lo! in the des-ert rich flowers are springing, Streams ever co-pious are gliding a - long;
4. See, from all lands, from the isles of the o-cean, Praise to Je - ho - vah as-cending on high;

Hushed be the accents of sor-row and mourning, Zi - on in triumph begins her mild reign.
Hail to the millions from bondage re-turn-ing, Gen-tiles and Jews the blest vis-ion be - hold.
Loud from the mountain-tops echoes are ring-ing, Wastes rise in verdure, and mingle in song.
Fall'n are the engines of war and com-mo-tion, Shouts of sal - va-tion are rend-ing the sky.

CAROLS.—In Shakespeare's time carols were sung in the streets at night during Christmas by the waits or watches, who expected to receive gifts for their singing. Many a writer upon old times and customs refers to the "wakeful ketches of Christmas Eve." It was after the Reformation that they ceased to sing Latin hymns in the churches, and substituted the sweet Christmas carols. There were then two kinds of carols in vogue—those of a devotional nature, which were sung not only in the churches, but also through the streets from house to house upon Christmas Eve,

and even after that, morning and evening, until Twelfth Day; for in those times men were able to spare more than one brief day for the celebration of Christmas, and often kept up the festival for some twelve days. Other carols were of a livelier nature, and were especially adapted to the revel and the feast where the lord of misrule had potent sway. These carols were all called wassail songs, and probably originated among the Anglo-Normans, who were of a convivial nature. No Christmas entertainment was complete without the joyous singing of carols, and

COME, WITH THY LUTE.

GERMAN MELODY.

Moderato.

1. Come, with thy lute, to the fount - ain; Sing me a song of the moun-tain;
2. Come, where the zeph-yrs are stray - ing, Where, 'mid the flow - er-buds play - ing,
3. Why should we droop in our sad - ness, Na - ture, her prom - ise of glad - ness

Sing of the hap - py and free, There, while the ray is de - clin - ing,
Rambles the blithe summer bee; Let the lone churl, in his sor - row,
Sheds o - ver land and o'er sea; Come, bring thy lute to the foun - tain,

While its last ro - ses are shin - ing, Sweet shall our mel - o - dies be,
He who despairs of the mor - row, Far to his sol - i - tude flee,
Sing, love, a song of the moun - tain, Sweet shall our mel - o - dies be,

Un - der the broad lin - den tree, Un - der the broad lin - den tree.
Un - der the dark cy - press tree, Un - der the dark cy - press tree.
Un - der the broad lin - den tree, Un - der the broad lin - den tree.

Un - der the lin - den tree, Un - der the lin - den tree.
2. cy - press   2. cy - press

thence came the rule; "No song, no supper," for every guest at the table was expected to join in the carol. One of the old rules was that "the ancient master of the revel is, after dinner and supper, to sing a carol, or song, and to command the other gentlemen present to sing with him and the companies."

WHEN simple curiosity passes into love of knowledge as such, and the gratification of the æsthetic sense of the beauty of completeness and accuracy seems more desirable than the easy indolence of ignorance; when the finding out of the causes of things becomes a source

of joy, and he is accounted happy who is successful in the search, common knowledge passes into what has been called natural history, whence there is but a step to that which now passes by the name of physical science. In this final state of knowledge, the phenomena of nature are regarded as a continuous series of causes and effects. And the ultimate object of science is to trace that series, from the term which is nearest us to that which is at the farthest limit accessible to our means of investigation. The field of Nature is boundless, nowhere inaccessible, everywhere unfathomable.

IN instrumental music, even more than in singing, much depends on the fidelity and earnestness of the pupil. It is true that if the lesson be very long and intricate, it is not possible for each pupil to play it through with close criticism; but individual performance is not the most important part of teaching; we are all more or less imitative, and learn by example and precept, by the mistakes and successes of others. Number six on Monday should be number one on Thursday, and in turn become a model or a beacon. The stimulus that is assumed by the associating of pupils in this work is too important to be overlooked. Apart from that instinct in human nature manifested in a desire to excel and surpass others in any contest, the habit of playing and singing in the presence of others tends to banish shyness; and that wretched *mauvaise honte* which many of us know to our cost keeps silent many a music lover who, it may be, is no mean performer, but, unused to displaying his or her talent before others than the teacher, is overwhelmed with fright when asked to confer pleasure, getting only a partial and individual enjoyment out of a large expenditure of time and money.

VIVA L'AMERICA.

H. MILLARD.
By per. WM. A. POND & CO.

Declamato.

1. No - ble Re - pub - lic! happiest of lands! Fore-most of na - tions Colum - bia stands.
2. Should ev - er trai - tor rise in the land, Curs'd be his home-stead, wither'd his hand;
3. To all her he - roes, jus - tice, and fame; To all her foes, a traitor's foul name;

Freedom's proud ban - ner floats in the skies! Where shouts of Lib - er - ty
Shame be his mem - 'ry, scorn be his lot, Ex - ile his her - i - tage,
Our stripes and stars still proud - ly shall wave, Em - blem of Lib - er - ty—

dai - ly arise! U - nit - ed we stand, di - vided we fall, Union for - ev - er, freedom for all;
his name a blot. U - nit - ed we stand, di - vided we fall, Granting a home and freedom to all;
Flag of the brave! U - nit - ed we stand, di - vided we fall, Gladly we'll die at our country's call;

Chorus.

Throughout the world, our mot - to shall be, Vi - va l'Amer - i - ca, Home of the Free!

IN the spring of 1863 two great armies encamped on either side of the Rappahannock River, one in blue and the other in gray. One evening, as twilight fell, the bands of music on the Union side began to play their martial music, the "Star Spangled Banner" and "Rally Round the Flag;" and that challenge of music was taken up by those upon the other side, who responded with the "Bonnie Blue Flag" and "Away Down South in Dixie." It was borne in upon the soul of a single soldier in one of those army bands to begin a sweeter and more tender air, and slowly, as he played it, they joined in a sort of chorus of all the instruments upon the Union side, until finally a great and mighty tide of harmony swelled up and down our army—"Home, Sweet Home." When that band finished there was no challenge yonder, for every band upon that farther shore had taken up the lovely air, so attuned to all that is holiest and dearest, and one grand chorus of the two great hosts went up to God. When they had finished, from the boys in gray came a challenge, "Three cheers for home!" and as they went resounding through the skies from both sides of the river, "something upon the soldiers' cheeks washed off the stains of powder."— *Frances E. Willard.*

BALLADS.—The conditions under which our ancient ballad-poetry arose are tolerably well understood. It belongs to a primitive state of society, in which the knowledge of letters was restricted to a select class, and tradition was the sole vehicle of history to the mass of the people; when manners were ruder, laws less reverenced, the passions more unbridled, the utterance of emotion franker and less conventional than now. Though the writers cannot always be supposed contemporary with the events they record, they uniformly address a sympathetic audience, whose standard of morality or sentiment, and level of culture, little, if at all, differ from those prevailing at the period to which their traditions refer. The Border minstrelsy, for example, was obviously written for the children or grandchildren of the moss-troopers whose exploits it glorifies, a generation to whom appeals to a higher code or a purer taste than their ancestors accepted would have been wholly unintelligible. The general characteristics of the best specimens that remain to us, whether of the narrative and legendary ballad or of the lyrical and emotional ballad, are an unconscious simplicity of thought and language, a coarse but vivid realization of the scenes and delineation of the personages presented. They show few marks of artistic construction

COME AGAIN.

1. We will take from our parting its bitterest word, No adieu shall be spoken, no farewell be heard, And our
2. Come again, come again, with a warm, loving heart, We have met with a smile, with a smile let us part, [Tho' the

last fond embrace shall be eas'd of its pain, By those sweet, soothing words, Come again, come again. Well we
bright, smiling day of our meeting may wane, We will sing when we part, Come again, come again. Then give

know when we sever, the tear and the sigh Will be heaving the breast and o'erflowing the eye, But the
us the hand, though the world may be wide, And the deep rolling ocean so soon may divide; Where'er

beam thro' the tear-drop shall kindle amain, And the sigh ech-o back, Come again, come again.
we may wander, o'er land or o'er main, Hope shall whisper the words, Come again, come again.

or ornament, beyond a rudimentary sense of pictorial expression, and the occasional introduction of abrupt snatches of wild fancy. In those cases where a burden is added, it serves either to mark the leading motive of the theme, to suggest the musical accompaniment to which the piece was set, or that "rhythm of the feet" from which the composition first took its name. The impossibility of restoring the conditions under which this description of poetry arose, does not oppose any obstacle to its successful cultivation in our day. To surrender the type would be a gratuitous waste of means, for of all narrative and lyrical forms, it is the simplest and the most direct in its effects. The testimony borne to its potency by Sir Philip Sidney, by Addison, and the authority for whom Fletcher of Saltoun stood sponsor, would be unanimously endorsed to-day. The varnish of our social conventionalism is, after all, extremely thin, and the most cultivated audience cannot listen to a plain story of heroism or of pathos without flushing cheeks and burning eyes. For enshrining the memory of any grandly heroic achievement, for giving utterance to any pure emotion, the ballad remains the most appropriate vehicle.—*Contemporary Review.*

THE DANUBE RIVER.

Tempo di Mazurka.

HAMILTON AIDE.

1. Do you re-call that night in June, Up-on the Dan-ube riv-er? We
2. Our boat kept meas-ure with its oar, The mus-ic rose in snatch-es; From

listened to a Länd-ler tune, And watched the moonbeams quiver. I oft since then have
peasants danc-ing on the shore, With boist-rous songs and catches. I know not why that

rit. *a tempo.*

watched the moon, But nev-er, no, Oh nev-er, nev-er, Can I for-get that
Länd-ler rang Thro' all my soul, But nev-er, nev-er, Can I for-get. the

night in June, Up-on the Dan-ube riv-er, Can I for-get that night in June, Up-
songs they sang, Up-on the Dan-ube riv-er, Can I for-get the songs they sang Up-

on the Dan-ube riv-er, Can I for-get that night in June, Up-on the Dan-ube
on the Dan-ube riv-er, Can I for-get the songs they sang, Up-on the Dan-ube

riv-er, Can I for-get that night in June, Up-on the Dan-ube riv-er.
riv-er, Can I for-get the songs they sang, Up-on the Dan-ube riv-er.

JEANNETTE AND JEANNOT.

CHAS. JEFFREYS.
CHAS. W. GLOVER.

Moderato.

1. You are go-ing far a-way, Far a-way from poor Jeannette, There is
2. Or when glo-ry leads the way, You'll be mad-ly rush-ing on, Nev-er

no one left to love me now, And you too may for-get; But my
think-ing, if they kill you, that My hap-pi-ness is gone: If you

heart will be with you, Wher-ev-er you may go, Can you
win the day, perhaps, A gen-er-al you'll be, Tho' I'm

look me in the face, And say the same, Jean-not? When you
proud to think of that, What will be-come of me? Oh! if

wear the jack-et red, And the beau-ti-ful cockade, Oh, I fear you will for-
I were Queen of France, Or, still bet-ter, Pope of Rome, I would have no fight-ing

get All the prom-is-es you've made; With your gun up-on your shoulder, And your
men a-broad, No weep-ing maids at home; All the world should be at peace, Or if

bay'-net by your side, You'll be tak-ing some proud la-dy, And be mak-ing her your
kings must show their might, Why, let them who make the quar-rels Be the on-ly men to

bride; You'll be tak-ing some proud la-dy, And be mak-ing her your bride.
fight; Yes, let them who make the quar-rels Be the on-ly men to fight.

THEN YOU'LL REMEMBER ME.

M. W. BALFE.

Andante cantabile.

1. When oth-er lips and oth-er hearts Their tales of love shall tell, In
2. When cold-ness or de-ceit shall slight The beau-ty now they prize, And

lan-guage whose ex-cess im-parts The pow'r they feel so well, There
deem it but a fad-ed light Which beams with-in your eyes; When

may, per-haps, in such a scene Some rec-ol-lec-tion be Of days that have as
hol-low hearts shall wear a mask 'Twill break your own to see: In such a moment

hap-py been, And you'll re-member me, And you'll remember, you'll remember me.
I but ask, That you'll re-member me, That you'll remember, you'll remember me.

"THESE musicians are a queer set; it is hard to please them; it is hard to get along with them!" This and similar expressions one hears every now and then from the lips of people who think they know of what they speak. We will lay down a few rules of etiquette for the benefit of such; they may get 'along better with musicians by learning a lesson from them. When you invite a musician to dine with you, give him at once to understand that you expect him to entertain your company. Any man of self-respect will appreciate such an invitation. If he comes and does play, be sure to start a lively discussion while he is at the piano, for this is a compliment that cannot fail to please him. When he has played his selections, tell him how you enjoyed the performance of this or that great pianist or singer, who perchance performed the same pieces. It places the musician in a favorable light, and makes him feel comfortable, or, if you please, enter a complaint against the style of his music, either that it is too classic, or too popular, for this shows that you are a man of good taste and judgment. If you are acquainted among the musicians of your town, criticise those that are absent; it is reasonable to suppose that he indulges in like unfavorable opinions of other musicians and that he will be pleased with your remarks. If you have a very difficult piece on hand, ask him to play it at sight, for what sort of a musician is he who cannot play everything at sight? When a musician refuses to play, keep

CLEAR THE WAY.

SCHOOL SONGS.

Allegretto.

1. The stars are fad - ing from the sky, The mists be - fore the morning fly; The
2. The cock has crowed with all his might, The birds are sing - ing with de - light, The
3. The bell is ring - ing, haste a - way; The school is o - pen, leave off play; The

east is glow - ing with a smile, And na - ture laughing all the while, Says,
hum of busi - ness meets the ear, And face to face, with kind - ly cheer, Says,
sun of knowledge there we find, A - ris - ing on the youth - ful mind; So,

Clear the way! the world is wak - ing, Clear the way! the world is wak ing,

Clear the way! the world is wak - ing, Night is gone, and day is breaking!

on asking him, for his refusal is only a pretense. It is true you would not press a man to eat if he declined, but then there is a difference between eating and playing. A musician ought always to be ready to play, no matter how he feels. Of course, you would not think of asking a lawyer who dines with you for an opinion in a case that involves a lawsuit, nor would you ask a physician to prescribe for your child while you socially entertained him, for these people charge for their professional labor; but why should a musician refuse to give you and your company the benefit of his skill? His work is only play, that's all. If he views the matter from a different standpoint, denounce him as selfish and mean, and do what you can to injure his business among your friends. When you expect a musician to play for you, don't take the trouble to have a tuner examine the condition of your piano. What if it is out of tune! If you are satisfied with discords, the musician surely ought to be. It is different with painters; they must have good brushes and paints, to produce good pictures; a mechanic must have good tools to do good work, but a musician should make good music on any old trap of an organ or piano, whether in tune or not. One more rule: Everybody likes to be treated with a patronizing air, musicians especially. Let them feel your superiority socially and financially; treat them as a class who live on flattery, and must be indulged as children. This is the best way to get along with these queer people!—*Karl Merz.*

I HAVE here a simple apparatus to show that rapid and regular shocks produce a natural musical note. This wheel is milled at the edge, and when I turn it rapidly so that it strikes against the edge of the card fixed behind it, the notches strike in rapid succession, and produce a musical sound. We can also prove by this experiment that the quicker the blows are, the higher the note will be. I pull the string gently at first, and then more quickly, and you will notice that the note grows sharper and sharper till the movement begins to slacken, when the note goes down again. This is because the more rapidly the air is hit, the shorter are the waves it makes, and short waves give a high note. Let us examine this with two tuning forks. I strike one, and it sounds C, the third space in the treble; I strike the other, and it sounds A, the first leger line, five notes above C. I have drawn on this diagram an imaginary picture of these two sets of waves. You see that the A fork makes three waves, while the C fork makes only two. Why is this? Because the prong of the A fork moves three times backwards and forwards while the prong of the C fork moves only twice; therefore the A fork does not crowd so many atoms together before it draws back, and the waves are shorter. These two notes, C and A, are three-fourths of an octave apart; if we had two forks, one going twice as fast as the other, making four waves while the other made two, then that note would be an octave higher.—*Buckley.*

SEE WHERE THE RISING SUN.

FROM THE GERMAN.

Allegro.

1. See where the ris - ing sun, In splendor decks the skies, His daily course be - gun;
2. Fair is the face of morn; Why should your eyelids keep Closed, when the night is gone?

Fine.

Hast - en, a - rise! Oh, come with me where violets bloom, And fill the air with
Wake from your sleep! Oh, who would slumber in his bed, When darkness from his

D.C.

sweet perfume; And where, like diamonds to the sight, Dew - drops spar - kle bright,
couch has fled, And when the lark is soar - ing high, And warbling songs of joy?

1 (ROUND.)   2

Dress a bad boy up in gold - lace if you will, And yet he will be but a

3

bad boy still, And yet he will be but a bad boy still.

1 (ROUND.)   2

To the praise of truth, to the praise of truth we sing, To the

3

praise of truth, to the praise of truth we sing, For the truth is a no - ble thing.

INSIDE that curled part of the labyrinth, which looks like a snail-shell and is called the *cochlea*, there is a most wonderful apparatus of more than three thousand fine stretched filaments or threads, and these act like the strings of a harp, and make us hear different tones. If we go near to a harp or a piano, and sing any particular note very loudly, we may hear this note sounding in the instrument, because we will set just that particular string quivering which gives the note we sang. The air-waves set going by the voice touch that string, because it can quiver in time with them, while none of the other strings can do so. Now, just in the same way the tiny instrument of three thousand strings in the ear, which is called Corti's organ, vibrates to the air-waves, one thread to one set of waves, another to another, and according to the fibre that quivers, will be the sound we hear. Here, then, we see how nature speaks to us. All the movements going on outside, however violent and varied they may be, cannot of themselves make sound. But here, in this little space behind the drum of our ear, the air-waves are sorted and sent on to our brain, where they speak as sound.

THE Bible contains the songs and prophecies that burst from human souls when the moral idea first dawned upon them in all its sublime grandeur; and those first expressions of astonishment, enthusiasm and self-forgetful love have never been equalled by any subsequent expressions for freshness and might.—*Adlar.*

THAT DAY THE WORLD SHALL SEE.

W. E. HICKSON.
J. W. CALLCOTT.

Lively.

1. May ev - 'ry year but bring more near The time when strife shall cease, And truth and love all hearts shall move To live in joy and peace. Now sor - row reigns, and earth complains, For fol - ly still her power maintains; But the day shall yet ap - pear, When the might with the right and the truth shall be, When the might with the right and the truth shall be, And come what there may to stand in the way, That day the world shall see.

2. Let good men ne'er of truth des - pair, Though humble ef - forts fail; Oh, give not o'er, un - til once more The righteous cause pre - vail; In vain, 'mid long en - dur - ing wrong, The weak may strive against the strong; But the day will sure - ly come,

be,...

AULD LANG SYNE is popularly supposed to be the composition of Burns, but, in fact, he wrote only the second and third verses of the ballad as commonly sung, retouching the others from an older and less familiar song. The Old Oaken Bucket was written by Woodworth, in New York City, during the hot summer of 1817. He came into the house and drank a glass of water, and then said, "How much more refreshing it would be to take a good, long drink from the old oaken bucket that used to hang in my father's well." His wife suggested that it was a happy thought for a poem. He sat down and wrote the song as we have it. Woodman, Spare that Tree! was the result of an incident that came to the knowledge of George

P. Morris. A friend's mother had owned a little place in the country, which she was obliged, from poverty, to sell. On the property grew a large oak which had been planted by his grandfather. The purchaser of the house and land proposed to cut down the tree, and Morris's friend paid him ten dollars for a bond that the oak should be spared. Morris heard the story, saw the tree, and wrote the song. Oft in the Stilly Night was produced by Moore after his family had undergone, apparently, every possible misfortune; one of his children died young, another went astray, and a third was accidentally killed. The Light of Other Days was written for Balfe's opera, the "Maid of Artois." The opera is forgotten, but the song still lives, and is as popular as ever.

SMILING MAY COMES IN PLAY.

1. Smil-ing May comes in play   Making all things bright and gay, From the hill come ye all
2. As   we   stray, breezes play,   Through the fair grove's fresh array, All is bright to   the   sight,

To the flowers sweet that call; Fragrant is the flow'ry vale, Sparkles now the dew-bright dale;
Gone a - far   is winter's night; Shadows now all quiv'ring glance, In the silv'ry fountain's dance,

Mu - sic floats in soft notes From sweet warbler's throats Singing merrily, mer-ri - ly, mer-ri - ly,
Insects bright sport in light, Charming   to the sight; Sporting merrily, mer-ri - ly, mer-ri - ly,

Singing merri-ly, merri-ly, merri-ly, Mu - sic floats in soft notes From sweet warbler's throats.
Sporting merri-ly, merri-ly, merri-ly, Insects bright sport in light, Charm-ing to the sight.

[Or this Movement Song.]

Here we stand,	Right hand up,	Seated now,
Hand in hand,	Left hand up;	Smooth your brow,
Ready for our exercise;	Whirling see our fingers go!	Then drum lightly on your crown
Heads upright,	Folded now,	Oh, what fun!
With delight	Let us bow	Every one
Sparkling in our laughing eyes!	Gently to each other so!	Driving off each surly frown!
Singing cheerily,	Eastward point,	Quickly stand,
Cheerily, cheerily,	Westward point;	Lungs expand,
Clapping merrily, merrily, merrily,	Left hand Nadir, Zenith right;	Backward let our shoulders go!
One, two, three,	Forward fold,	Life and health,
Don't you see	Backward fold;	Comfort, wealth,
Where scholars love to be?	Arms akimbo, chest upright;	We can thus improve, you know.

MILITARY MUSIC.—The origin of military music takes us back to remote antiquity. Every nation in ancient times had its peculiar instruments of music, and its national songs. These songs invariably refer to victories gained, battles fought, sieges carried on, or the services of some individual hero. The name of the soldier or officer who had done some deed of renown stood beside that of the general who commanded. With the Spartans, the song Castor was the signal for combat; the Romans took cities to the sound of the trumpet and the horn; the Egyptians, Arabians and ancient Germans went to battle to the beating of drums, the sound of the flute, the cymbal and the clarion. In ancient times and among different people, each instrument had its peculiar use. The Chinese, in their war music, employed bells and triangles. With the Romans, the trumpet indicated the assembling of the troops, the bugle announced the coming of the general, and the horn gave the signal of retreat. It was to the noise of these instruments combined—discordant, shrill, deafening—that they threw themselves upon the ranks of the enemy. Among the Egyptians, bells, in conjunction with timbrels, served to form a species of military harmony. The Hebrew soldiery employed the horn, the trumpet, the timbrel and the sackbut, an instrument some-

NEVER SAY FAIL.

School-Day Singer.

1. Keep work-ing, 'tis wis-er than sit-ting a-side; Nev-er, oh, nev-er say fail!
2. In life's ros-y morn-ing, in manhood's fair pride, Nev-er, oh, nev-er say fail!

And dreaming, and sigh-ing, and wait-ing the tide; Nev-er, oh, nev-er say fail!
Let this be your mot-to, your foot-steps to guide, Nev-er, oh, nev-er say fail!

In life's earn-est bat-tle they on-ly pre-vail, Who dai-ly march on-ward and
In storm and in sun-shine what-ev-er as-sail, Push on-ward and con-quer, and

nev-er say fail! Nev-er say fail! Nev-er say fail! Nev-er, oh, nev-er say fail!
nev-er say fail! Nev-er say fail! Nev-er say fail! Nev-er, oh, nev-er say fail!

what resembling the trombone. The music attached to the Roman legions had made much progress at the time of the conquest of the Gauls; but dating from this epoch, it became more and more feeble. The soldiery of France received and preserved the clarion and trumpet of Cæsar's armies, but the custom of making use of music was insensibly lost. At the commencement of the Middle Ages, the instruments handed down and preserved were useful merely in rallying the soldiers, calling them to battle, and making them endure with gayety the fatigues of a march. At this time, the method of the Romans had entirely disappeared. About this period, the French min- strels began occasionally to accompany the troops to battle. Their instruments were the rebec, a little three-stringed violin, bagpipe, and flute or pipe. About the year 1330, they began to use the clarion, an instrument derived from the Moors, who transmitted it into Portugal from Africa. The cornet, another war instrument of the ancients, made its reappearance about the same time. It was about this time, also, that the adventurous Italian bands recovered the usage of military music, which soon spread among the other nations of Europe. To the drums and trumpets they joined the flute, fife and pandean pipe The drum was played with a single stick.—*Moore.*

AWAY TO SCHOOL.

GERMAN AIR.

Lively.

mf   *f*

1. Our youth-ful hearts for learn-ing burn; A - way, a way to school; To sci - ence now our
2. Be - hold a hap - py band ap - pears; A - way, a - way to school; The shout of joy now
3. No more we roam in i - dle play; A - way, a - way to school; In stu - dy now we

cres -

steps we turn; A - way, a - way to school. We turn from home and all its charms, And
fills our ears; A - way, a - way to school. Our voi - ces ring in mus - ic sweet, When
spend the day; A - way, a - way to school. U - ni - ted in a peace - ful band, We're

cen - do.   *f*

leave our pa - rents' lov - ing arms; ⎫
with our friends in school we meet; ⎬ Away to school, a - way to school, A - way, a - way to school.
join'd in heart, we're join'd in hand; ⎭

MUSIC EVERYWHERE.

S. W. FOSTER.

Not too slow.

1. Mu - sic in the val - ley, Mu-sic on the hill,   Mu - sic in the woodland, Music in the rill;
2. Mu - sic by the fire-side, Mu-sic in the hall,   Mu - sic in the school-room, Music for us all;
3. Sing with joyful voi- ces, Friends and lov'd ones dear, Let no jarring discord Ev - er en-ter here;

f

Mu - sic on the mountain, Music in the air,   Mu - sic in the true heart, Music ev-'rywhere.
Mu - sic in our sor-row, Music in our care,   Mu - sic in our glad-ness, Music ev-'rywhere.
Join the happy cho - rus Of all na-ture fair,   Swell the glorious an-them, Music ev-'rywhere.

11—L

TROIKA, RUSSIAN DRIVER'S SONG.

CARL MATZ ARR.

Andantino.

1. The post-house lamp had died away, And in the fire expir'd the light; Strange visions o'er my fancy play, And sleep o'ertakes my weary sight, Strange visions o'er my fancy play, And sleep o'ertakes my weary sight: A youthful driver, roused at night, Seemed in a dream, and slowly moved; He sang of eyes so beaming bright, The beauteous eyes of her he loved, "Oh, those blue eyes, those eyes of blue, They've broke a gallant spirit's ease; Oh! cruel fate, 'twas hard of you, To tear asunder hearts like

2. Three noble horses swiftly fly, Along the smooth broad road they go; The bell, the gift of our Valdai, Sounds mournfully beneath the bow, The bell, the gift of our Valdai, Sounds mournfully beneath the bow. The youth had said his last farewell, And madly now pursued his way; Yet louder than the tinkling bell You still might hear his plaintive lay, "Oh, those blue eyes, those eyes of blue, They've broke a gallant spirit's

mp

these! Oh, cru - el fate, 'twas hard of you, To tear a - sun - der hearts like these!"

WHEN STARS ARE IN THE QUIET SKIES.

EDWARD LYTTON BULWER.

1. When stars are in the qui - et skies, Then most I pine for
2. There is an hour when an - gels keep Fa - mil - iar watch on
3. The thoughts of thee too sa - cred are For day - light's com - mon

thee; Bend on me then thy ten - der eyes, As stars look on the
men, When coars - er souls are wrapped in sleep, Sweet spir - it, meet me
beam; I can but know thee as my star, My an - gel, and my

sea! For thoughts, like waves that glide by night, Are still - est when they
then. There is an hour when ho - ly dreams Thro' slum - ber, fair - est,
dream! When stars are in the qui - et skies, Then most I pine for

shine; Mine earthly love lies hush'd in light Be - neath the heav'n of
glide, And in that mys - tic hour it seems Thou shouldst be by my
thee; Bend on me then thy ten - der eyes, As stars look on the

ad lib.

thine, Mine earthly love lies hush'd in light Beneath the heav'n of thine.
side, And in that mys - tic hour it seems Thou shouldst be by my side.
sea, Bend on me then thy ten - der eyes, As stars look on the sea.

EVANGELINE.

WILL S. HAYS,
By per. S. BRAINARD'S SONS.

1. Sweet E - van - geline, My lost E - van - geline, We have lived and loved each other
2. I am lonely now, My dear E - van - geline, The days are long, the nights are

fond and true, Ev - er true to thee, tho' far a - way I've been, My
sad and drear, And how changed, a - las! each well re - membered scene, Since

heart has ev - er dwelt with you, But O, those hap - py days will
you and I were sit - ting here, A - las! you nev - er - more will

rit. ∧ ∧ ∧ ∧ *a tempo.*

ne'er re - turn, Those hap - py days that we have seen, For
smile on me, And life is now a sad, sad dream, I

I am left to weep a - lone, My sweet E - van - ge - line,
lived to love none else but thee, My sweet E - van - ge - line.

Chorus.

Oh! how sad we've been, lost E - van - ge - line, Since we laid thee where the sweetest flowers wave, And the an - gels bright, Robed in spot - less white, Are

She is gone, yes, she is gone, yes! she is gone,

watching o'er thy green and mos - sy grave. E - van - geline, E - van - geline, E -

E - van - ge - line,

lento.

van - ge - line, E - van - ge - line, To the si - lent grave.

pp

She's gone,

OVER THE MOUNTAIN WAVE.

E. L. WHITE.

1. O - ver the mountain wave See where they come; Storm-cloud and wint'ry wind Welcome them home;
2. Dim grew the for - est path, Onward they trod; Firm beat their noble hearts, Trust - ing in God!
3. Not theirs the glory-wreath, Torn by the blast; Heav'nward their holy steps, Heavenward they passed.

Yet where the sounding gale Howls to the sea, There their song peals along, Deep-toned and free :
Gray men and blooming maids, High rose their song, Hear it sweep, clear and deep, Ever a - long :
Green be their mos-sy graves, Ours be their fame, While their song peals along Ever the same :

Chorus.

" Pilgrims and wanderers, Hith - er we come; Where the free dare to be, There is our home."

LIFE-SOUNDS.—We think for a moment of life-sounds, of which there are so many around us. Do you know why we hear a buzzing, as the gnat, the bee, or the cockchafer fly past? Not by the beating of their wings against the air, as many people imagine, and as is really the case with humming birds, but by the scraping of the under-part of their hard wings against the edges of their hind-legs, which are toothed like a saw. The more rapidly their wings are put in motion the stronger this grating sound becomes. Some insects, like the drone-fly, force the air through the tiny air-passages in their sides, and as these passages are closed by little plates, the plates vibrate to and fro and make sound-waves. All these life-sounds are made by creatures which do not sing or speak; but the sweetest sounds of all in the woods are the voices of the birds. All voice-sounds are made by two elastic bands or cushions, called vocal chords, stretched across the end of the tube or windpipe through which we breathe, and as we send the air through them we tighten or loosen them as we will, and so make them vibrate quickly or slowly and make sound-waves of different lengths. But if you will try some day in the woods you will find that a bird can

JUANITA.

SPANISH MELODY,
Words by MRS. NORTON.

mf

1. Soft o'er the fountain, Ling'ring falls the south-ern moon; Far o'er the mountain
2. When in thy dreaming, Moons like these shall shine a-gain, And daylight beaming,

Breaks the day too soon! in thy dark eye's splendor, Where the warm light loves to dwell,
Prove thy dreams are vain. Wilt thou not, re-lent-ing, For thine ab-sent lov-er sigh,

Slower. *A tempo.*

p *mf*

Wea-ry looks, yet ten-der, Speak their fond fare-well! Ni-ta! Jua-ni-ta! *
In thy heart con-sent-ing To a prayer gone by? Ni-ta! Jua-ni-ta!

Tenderly. rit.

pp

Ask thy soul if we should part! Ni-ta! Jua-ni-ta! Lean thou on my heart.
Let me lin-ger by thy side! Ni-ta! Jua-ni-ta! Be my own fair bride!

* Wah-ne-ta.

surpass you over and over again in the length of his note; when you are out of breath and forced to stop he will go on with his merry trill as fresh and clear as if he had only just begun. This is because birds can draw air into the whole of their body, and they have a large stock laid up in the folds of their windpipe, and besides this the air-chamber behind their elastic bands or vocal chords has two compartments where we have only one, and the second compartment has special muscles by which they can open and shut it, and so prolong the trill. Only think what a rapid succession of waves must quiver through the air as a tiny bird agitates his little throat and pours forth a volume of song! The next time you can do so, spend half-an-hour listening to him, or to the canary bird as he swings in his cage, and try to picture to yourself how that little being is moving all the atmosphere around him. Then dream for a little while about Sound, what it is, how marvelously it works outside in the world, and inside in your ear and brain; and then, when you go back to work again, you will hardly deny that it is well worth while to listen sometimes to the voices of Nature and ponder how it is that we hear them.—*Miss A. R. Buckley*

THE BLUE ALSATIAN MOUNTAINS.

Stephen Adams.
Claribel. C. Matz Arr.

Not too slow.

1. By the blue Al - sa - tian mountains Dwelt a maiden young and fair, Like the careless · flow - ing
2. By the blue Al - sa - tian mountains Came a stranger in the Spring, And he lin-ger'd by the
3. By the blue Al - sa - tian mountains Many spring-times bloom'd and pass'd, And the maiden by the

foun-tains Were the rip - ples of her hair, Were the rip - ples of her hair; An-gel
foun-tains Just to hear the maid-en sing, Just to hear the maid-en sing; Just to
foun-tains, Saw she lost her hopes at last, She lost her hopes at last. And she

mild her eyes so win-ning, Angel bright her hap - py smile, When be - neath the fountains spin-
whis-per in the moonlight, Words the sweetest she had known, Just to charm a - way the hours,
withered like a flow - er That is wait-ing for the rain, She will never see the stranger,

ning, You could hear her song the while. A - dé, A - dé, A - dé, Such songs will pass away,
Till her heart was all his own. A - dé, A - dé, A - dé, Such dreams may pass away,
Where the fountains fall a gain. A - dé, A - dé, A - dé, The years have passed away,

Chorus.

Tho' the blue Al-sa-tian moun-tains Seem to watch and wait alway,
But the blue Al - sa-tian moun-tains Seem to watch and wait alway.
But the blue Al - sa-tian moun-tains Seem to watch and wait alway. A - dé, A - dé, A - dé
[A - day,]

Such songs will pass away, Tho' the blue Alsa-tian mountains Seem to watch and wait alway.

JOHNNY SANDS.

John Sinclair.

mp

1. A man whose name was Johnny Sands, Had married Betty Hague, And though she brought him
2. "For fear that I should cour-age lack, And try to save my life, Pray, tie my hands be-

gold and lands, She proved a ter-ri-ble plague; For, oh, she was a scold-ing wife, Full
hind my back," "I will," re-plied his wife, She tied them fast, as you may think, And

of ca-price and whim, He said that he was tired of life, And she was tired of
when se-cure-ly done, "Now stand," she says, "upon the brink, And I'll pre-pare to

mp

him, And she was tired of him, And she was tired of him; Says
run, And I'll pre-pare to run, And I'll pre-pare to run." All

f

he, "Then I will drown myself, The riv-er runs be-low;" Says she, "Pray do, you
down the hill his lov-ing bride Now ran with all her force, To push him in— he

sil-ly elf, I wished it long a-go." Says he, "Up-on the brink I'll stand, Do
stepped aside, And she fell in, of course; Now splash-ing, dash-ing, like a fish, "Oh,

you run down the hill, And push me in with all your might." Says she, "My love, I
save me, John-ny Sands." "I can't, my dear, tho' much I wish, For you have tied my

will," Says she, "My love, I will," Says she, "My love, I will."
hands, For you have tied my hands, For you have tied my hands."

WE'D BETTER BIDE A WEE.

CLARIBEL.

mf

1. The puir auld folk at hame, ye mind, Are frail and fail-ing sair, And weel I ken they'd
2. When first we told our sto-ry, lad, Their bless-ing fell sae free, They gave no thought to
3. I fear me, sair, they're failing baith, For when I sit a - part, They'll talk o' Heav'n sae

miss me, lad, Gin I came hame nae mair. The grist is out, the times are hard, The
self at all, They did but think of me, But, lad - die, that's a time a - wa, And
earn - est - ly, It well-nigh breaks my heart! So, lad - die, din - na urge me mair, It

kine are on - ly three,
mith - er's like to dee,   } I can - na leave the auld folk now, We'd bet-ter bide a
sure - ly win - na be,

wee, I can - na leave the auld folk now, We'd bet-ter bide a wee.

THE greatest privilege of a city life seems to be its musical opportunities. In the cultivated or mountainous country a banquet is provided for the eye. And there, too, we can have intellectual pleasures—communion through books with the best minds, thoughts, and experiences of our own age and history. The city alone can give us a chorus, a sublime organ, and an orchestra. In these some of the rich and manifest advances of modern over ancient civilization are summed up. . . . Perhaps there is a music of the spheres, but we can only imagine it—we know nothing of it. I have sometimes thought that if a blind spirit could be supported in space so as to hear, as this globe rolled by him, the notes that are borne on it—the myriad-voiced melody of birds, the sweeping of winds over all the zones, and the sheets of sound, now sombre, now cheerful, they waken from the forests which they stir; the low, lisping penitence of the peaceful sea, and, through all, the thunderous mellow bass of the stirred ocean, beating on a thousand leagues of rock—that

KELVIN GROVE.

THOMAS LYLE.

Affetuoso.

1. Let us haste to Kel - vin Grove, Bon - nie las - sie O!
2. We will wan - der by the mill, Bon - nie las - sie O!
3. Oh, Kel - vin's banks are fair, Bon - nie las - sie O!

Through its ma - zes let us rove, Bon - nie las - sie, O!
To the cove be - side the rill, Bon - nie las - sie, O!
When in Sum - mer we are there, Bon - nie las - sie, O!

Where the rose in all its pride, Paints the hol - low din - gle side,
Where the glens re - bound the call, Of the lof - ty wa - ter - fall,
There the May pink's crim - son bloom Sheds a soft and sweet per - fume,

Where the mid - night fai - ries glide, Bon - nie las - sie O!
Thro' the moun - tain's rock - y hall, Bon - nie las - sie O!
Round the yel - low banks of broom, Bon - nie las - sie O!

spirit might imagine it was a mighty organ rolling by, touched on every key, alive in every stop, and aroused by every pedal to the praise of God. The highest music is religious. And, in speaking of orchestra, organ and chorus, as supplying the supreme civilized privilege of the city, let me go further and express my belief that the greatest fortune that can befall a person in the line of art is—more than seeing Rubens' picture of the Descent from the Cross, or Titian's Assumption, or Da Vinci's Last Supper, or Raffaelle's Transfiguration, or the Dresden Madonna—to hear Handel's "Messiah," when it is given with a competent combination of power and gifts. I always wonder, when I hear that oratorio, that in every city a grand cathedral service is not made out of it, or of selections from it, once a month, certainly every Christmas—that the promise of Christ, and the blessedness of his grace, and the beneficence of his reign, and glory of his triumph, may have fit interpretation in words and in ways that oversweep the petty divisions of catechisms and creeds.—*Rev. T. Starr King.*

UNISON.—When notes from any two sources are in unison, they are produced by the same number of vibrations. If the string of a violin, the cord of a guitar, the parchment of a drum, the pipe of an organ, produce the same musical tone, it is because the vibrations in all are performed in equal times. If a voice and a piano execute the same music, the steel strings of the piano and the vocal cords of the singer vibrate together and send out sound-waves of the same length.

In order, then, to determine the number and length of the sound-waves produced by a sonorous body, we have only to bring its sound and that of the *siren,* an instrument for determining the number of vibrations in a given time, into unison. In this way, says Tyndall, it has been found that the wings of a gnat flap, in flying, at the rate of 15,000 times per second. The waves of a man's voice in conversation are from 8 to 12 feet long; a woman's, from 2 to 4 feet long.

HUNTER'S FAREWELL.

MENDELSSOHN.
Arr. by CARL MATZ.

1. For - est fair, what might-y hand Hath in grand - eur thee cre - a - ted, With glad voice and heart e - la - ted Will I praise him who thee plann'd. . . . . heart e - la - ted Will I praise him who thee plann'd.

2. Toils the bus - y world be - low, Herds a - bove are peace-ful graz - ing, Let our horns and voi - ces rais - ing Make all hearts with joy o'er - flow. . . . . voi - ces rais - ing Make all hearts with joy o'er - flow.

3. What we joy - ful pledge to-day Let us ev - er faith - ful cher - ish, Nev - er shall re - membrance per - ish Till our last song dies a - way. . . . . membrance per - ish Till our last song dies a - way.

plann'd. With glad voice and flow. Let our horns and way. Nev - er shall re -

Fare thee well, ... Fare thee well,

1. 2. Fare thee well, thou for - est
3. God pro - tect thee, for - est

fair. 1. 2. Fare thee well, Fare thee well, thou for - est fair.
fair. 3. Fare thee well, God pro - tect thee, for - est fair.

ART OF SINGING.—It must have struck every intelligent frequenter of the concert-rooms to what hopeless straits an enthusiastic admirer of any particular singer is put when asked to give his reasons for appreciating the merits of his favorite. The answer, if one is given, is often couched in vague generalities, and in some cases may be said to amount to literally nothing at all. The artist has a good voice, one is told, a clear enunciation, has done some things very well or, it may be, his appearance and deportment are pleasing. Why should this incapacity to give a reason for liking a thing exist? The explanation is clear enough to those who have turned their attention to the phenomenon, and lies in the fact, that an audience taken collectively knows little or nothing of the art of singing, and even were the very party who is the object of applause interrogated as to the cause of his or her success, in but few cases probably would a satisfactory explanation be forthcoming, for although he or she may have received such education in the art as is usually afforded, that

LOVE'S YOUNG DREAM.

THOMAS MOORE.

Andantino.

1. Oh! the days are gone, when beau-ty bright My heart's chain wove; When my
2. Tho' the bard to pur-er flame may soar, When wild youth's past; Tho' he
3. Oh! that hal-lowed form is ne'er for-got, Which love first traced; Still it

dream of life, from morn till night, Was love, still love; New hope may bloom, and
win the wise, who frowned before, To smile at last; He'll nev-er meet a
linger-ing haunts the green-est spot On mem-'ry's waste! 'Twas o dor fled as

days may come Of mild-er, calm-er beam, But there's nothing half so sweet in life As
joy so sweet In all his noon of fame, As when first he sung to wo-man's ear His
soon as shed; 'Twas morning's winged dream! 'Twas a light that ne'er can shine a-gain On

love's young dream, Oh, there's nothing half so sweet in life As love's young dream.
soul-felt flame, And, at ev-'ry close, she blushed to hear The once-loved name.
life's dull stream! Oh, 'twas light that ne'er can shine a-gain On life's dull stream.

education does not take into account the fact that explanation may sometimes be required. There exists, indeed, no complete and intelligent system of vocal training. Pupils are not required to reason; suffice it if, after years of toil, by hook or by crook, rightly or wrongly, they acquire the power to produce certain effects. It may be pointed out as an extraordinary fact that, while singing is the most widely diffused of all arts, no art is more in its infancy with regard to the principles on which it is taught. We offer no explanation of the anomaly. A fine voice will go far with an uncritical audience, and there are many singers who set a higher value on the apparent satisfaction of others than on the absolute consciousness of having satisfied themselves.

THE interlude in the music is an echo, or a prophecy, or both combined. If it be an echo, it attempts to render in pure musical sound the dominant thought of the stanza that went before. If it be a prophecy, it sees what is coming and prepares the way for it, and brings the devotional congregation to the next stanza.

THE VOICE.—In the human system the parts concerned in the production of speech and music are three—the wind-pipe, the larynx, and the glottis. The windpipe is a tube which terminates in the lungs, through which the air passes to and from these organs. The larynx, which is essentially the organ of speech, is an enlargement of the upper part of the wind-pipe. The larynx terminates in two lateral membranes which approach to each other, having a little narrow opening between them called the glottis. The edges of these membranes form what are called the vocal chords. To produce voice the air expired from the lungs passes through the wind-pipe and out at the larynx through this opening between the membranes, the glottis; the vibration of the edges of these membranes, caused by the passage of air, produces sound. The organs of the voice produce sound on the same principles as a reed-instrument. By the action of delicate muscles we can vary the tension of these membranes, and make the opening between them large or

SEA-BIRD'S SONG.

VERDI.
JAMES SMITH.

1. Soaring in glee where the wa - ters rave, And the wild winds wail and sigh;
2. Rev-el - ing o'er the bil - lows vast, With hearts that nev - er fail;

Bound-ing a - far o'er the crest-ed wave That rolls to the stor - my sky;
Reefed sails may rend be - neath the blast, And the har - dy crew turn pale;

Swift as the flash of a sun - light beam, On with a wild - ly joyous scream,
Fear-less of dan - ger on we roam, O - ver our bound-less o-cean home,

Thun - der may roar, and light - ning gleam, Free as the winds we fly.
Beat - ing with joy the surg - ing foam, Brav-ing the roar - ing gale.

small, and thus render the tone of the voice grave or acute. The sound, as it passes through the mouth, is greatly modified by the tongue, teeth, lips, roof of mouth and nasal passages. The loudness of the voice depends mainly upon the force with which the air is expelled from the lungs. The force which a healthy chest can exert in blowing is about one pound per square inch of its surface; that is to say, the chest can condense its contained air with that force, and can blow through a tube, the mouth of which is ten feet under the surface of water. Coughing, sneezing, laughing, crying, each in itself a marvel of wonder, are due to the sudden expulsion of air from the lungs.

ALL persons cannot hear sound alike. In different individuals the sensibility of the auditory nerve varies greatly. The whole range of human hearing, from the lowest note of the organ to the highest known cry of insects, as of the cricket, includes about nine octaves.

SOME of the older and more familiar hymns which we have sung from our infancy, and the words of which we can repeat from beginning to end, yet without remembering ever to have committed them to memory, associate themselves so naturally with the inspired writings that it is almost with difficulty we can at all realize that these lines of living truth and of helpful love were actually written by mortals like ourselves,— poor erring mortals! many of them—in comparatively recent years. The hymn-writers of the last two centuries, those who have had the true gift from above, and who have used it with the right motive, have done more to aid and to elevate their fellow beings than they ever dreamed of doing, and are really only second to those who wrote under direct inspiration. In fact, however, who will venture to say that our hymnists have not been as directly and as truly inspired as were the evangelists themselves? Although, at first thought, it does require an effort of the mind, to realize that these hymns are the work of modern writers, it is very pleasant, and always a matter of interest, to know the incidents and circumstances of their composition..

THE RED, RED ROSE.

ROBERT BURNS.

1. Oh, my love is like the red, red rose, That's new-ly sprung in June, Oh, my love is like the
2. Till a' the seas gang dry, my dear, And the rocks melt wi' the sun, And I will love thee

mel - o - dy That's sweet-ly played in tune, As fair art thou, my bonnie lass, So
still, my dear, While the sands of life shall run, But fare-thee-weel, my on - ly love, And

deep in love am I, And I will love thee still, my dear, Till a' the seas gang dry. Till
fare-thee-weel a - while; And I will come again, my love, Tho' 'twere ten thousand miles, And

a' the seas gang dry, my dear, Till a' the seas gang dry, And I will love thee
I will come a - gain, my love, Tho' 'twere ten thousand miles, And I will come a -

2nd verse.

still, my dear, Till a' the seas gang dry.
gain, my love, Tho'... 'twere ten thou - sand miles.

THE absolute necessity of colleges of music was early discovered by the greatest musical peoples of the world, the Germans and Italians; and among the former especially we find to-day the most flourishing and extensive institutions of a musical educational character to be found in Europe. Mendelssohn, the founder of the Leipsic Conservatory, in reference to the class system of teaching, says: "An institution such as the conservatory has this advantage over the private instruction of the individual, that, by the participation of several in the same lessons at the same time, a true musical feeling is awakened and kept fresh among the people; it produces industry and spurs on to emulation; it is a preservative against one-sidedness of education and taste, a tendency against which every artist, even in the student years, should be upon his guard." No higher musical authority seems possible. When we add to it the result of that class system which every year brings before us in the accomplished graduates from those famous schools, it seems as if all carping criticism should be hushed.

FROM DAYS OF OLD.
(AUF WIEDERSEHN.)

FELIX MENDELSSOHN, 1839.

Poco Sostenuto.

1. It's been decreed from days of old, That, from the dearest man doth hold, There's part-ing.
2. To you is sent a bud to-day, You put it in a glass a-way Se - cure - ly.
3. And doth He give a love on earth, That thou dost prize as truly worth Thy keep - ing,

Although there's naught in life's ca-reer That falls so sad - ly on the ear, As
Next morn there blooms a love-ly rose, But fades be - fore the day doth close, So
It will but lit - tle time be thine; When gone, o'er loss thou'lt sad - ly pine, With

part - ing, Yes, part - ing. 4. Now must thou al - so well be-lieve,
sure - ly, Yes, sure - ly.
weep - ing, Yes, weep - ing.

Yes, well be-lieve, When of his friend man tak - eth leave, Then doth he say, "We'll
"Auf

meet a - gain! God keep us safe To meet a - gain!"
Wie - der-sehn! Auf Wie - der-sehn! Auf Wie - der - sehn!"

BAY OF DUBLIN

LADY DUFFERIN.

Sempre ad lib. con espressione.

1. Oh! Bay of Dub-lin! my heart you're troub-lin' Your beau-ty
2. Sweet Wick-low moun-tains! the sun-light sleep-ing On your green
3. How of-ten when at work, I'm sit-tin', And mus-in'

haunts me like a fe-ver dream— Like fro-zen foun-tains that the sun sets
banks is a pict-ure rare; You crowd a-round me like young girls
sad-ly on the days of yore, I think I see my Ka-tie

bub-blin', My heart's blood warms when I but hear your name; And nev-er
peep-in', And puz-zlin' me to say which is most fair; As tho' you'd
knit-tin' And the chil-der play-in' round the cab-in door; I think I

till this life-pulse ceas-es, My ear-liest, lat-est thought will cease to
see your own sweet fa-ces, Re-flect-ed in that smooth and sil-ver
see the neigh-bors' fa-ces, All gath-er'd round, their long-lost friend to

be, There's no-one here knows how fair that
sea, My bles-sin' on those love-ly
see! Tho' no one here knows how fair that

place is, And no one cares how dear it is to me.
pla-ces, Tho' no one cares how dear they are to me.
place is, Heav'n knows how dear my poor home was to me.

Wm. H. Keyser & Co., Music Typographers, 921 Arch St., Phila.

www.ingramcontent.com/pod-product-compliance
Lightning Source LLC
Chambersburg PA
CBHW020540270326
41927CB00006B/656

* 9 7 8 3 3 3 7 1 7 5 8 1 8 *